GOETHE'S SCIENCE
IN THE STRUCTURE OF THE *WANDERJAHRE*

GOETHE'S SCIENCE
IN THE STRUCTURE OF THE
WANDERJAHRE

A. G. STEER, JR.

THE UNIVERSITY OF GEORGIA PRESS
ATHENS

Paperback edition, 2008
© 1979 by the University of Georgia Press
Athens, Georgia 30602
www.ugapress.org
All rights reserved
Set in 11 on 12 point Mergenthaler Garamond type
Printed digitally in the United States of America

The Library of Congress has cataloged the hardcover edition
of this book as follows:
Library of Congress Cataloging-in-Publication Data
Steer, A. G. (Alfred Gilbert), 1913–
Goethe's science in the structure of the Wanderjahre /
A. G. Steer, Jr.
xi, 170 p. : ill. ; 23 cm.

ISBN 0-8203-0454-9
Includes index.
Bibliography: p. [157]-163.
1. Goethe, Johann Wolfgang von, 1749–1832. Wilhelm
Meisters Wanderjahre. 2. Goethe, Johann Wolfgang von,
1749–1832—Knowledge—Science. I. Title.
PT1982.A53 S7   833'.6   78-9886

Paperback ISBN-13: 978-0-8203-3261-1
ISBN-10: 0-8203-3261-5

FOR JEAN
AND OUR FAMILY

CONTENTS

	Preface	ix
I.	The Problem of Form	1
II.	The Narrative Insertions	9
III.	The Family as Archetype and Metamorphosis	17
IV.	"Saint Joseph the Second"	24
V.	"Die pilgernde Törin" (*The Foolish Woman on Pilgrimage*)	34
VI.	"Das nußbraune Mädchen" (*The Nut-brown Maid*)	39
VII.	"Wer ist der Verräter?" (*Who is the Traitor?*)	52
VIII.	"Der Mann von funfzig Jahren" (*The Man Fifty Years Old*)	58
IX.	Wilhelm's Prehistory	68
X.	"Die neue Melusine" (*The New Melusine*)	74
XI.	"Die gefährliche Wette" (*The Dangerous Bet*)	79
XII.	"Nicht zu Weit" (*Not Too Far*)	84
XIII.	The Nontitled Narrative Insertions	94
XIV.	Aphorisms, Maxims and Reflections	110
XV.	The Goethean Series	119
XVI.	The *Wanderjahre* as *Schlüsselroman*	126
XVII.	Conclusion	141
	Outline	144
	Notes	146
	Bibliography	157
	Index	164

PREFACE

AS IS WELL KNOWN, the second Wilhelm Meister novel, the *Wanderjahre*, failed to find an understanding audience in both the first and the final versions (1821 and 1829). Criticism and rejection were widespread, not only by contemporaries but also by most of the leading critics of the remainder of the nineteenth century as well. This was certainly no surprise to its author. Concerning the much less innovative *Lehrjahre*, he said in 1821 that his contemporaries "brauchten immer gehörige Zeit, bis sie ein vom Gewöhnlichen abweichendes Werk verdaut, sich zurechtgeschoben, genüglich reflektiert hätten."*[1] As he then knew, the *Wanderjahre* contained many more radical departures from tradition than the *Lehrjahre*, and thus would surely have an even harder time gaining acceptance. Sarter and Peschken have good summaries of the critical reception of the work, as do Anneliese Klingenberg and Heidi Gidion, so that there is no need to repeat them here.[2] One of the most recent and most influential negative voices was that of Emil Staiger, who said in 1959:[3] "Die Wanderjahre wurden zum Gefäß, in dem der Dichter alles Möglich zu unterbringen gedachte, was sich sonst in seinen Papieren verloren oder in unerfreulichen Einzelschriften verzettelt hätte."† Then he cited some of the undisputed errors that Goethe had permitted to creep into the final version, and went on: "Wir wissen, wie die einzelnen Teile zusammengefügt worden sind. An ein organisches Gebilde, klassische Mannigfaltigkeit ist da nicht zu denken."‡ So far Staiger had been repeating items of indictment

---

* always needed a good while until they had digested a work that deviated from the usual format, [until they had] adjusted it to suit themselves, reflected sufficiently [on it].

† The *Journeyman Years* became a receptacle into which the poet intended to put all possible sorts of things which otherwise would have been lost among his papers or would have been scattered in unappealing individual writings.

‡ We know how the individual parts were finally fitted together. Here there is no thought of organic formation, of classical manifoldness and unity.

leveled at Goethe by previous commentators, and he ended by citing another common reproach, namely that Goethe's powers were failing with old age: "Die Energie reicht nicht mehr aus, ein weitgedehntes Ganzes bestimmt und folgerichtig durchzubilden."*

However, beginning in the 1950s new and more positive voices began to make themselves heard in *Wanderjahre* scholarship. The most important of these was Erich Trunz, who in 1950, in the model introduction, commentary, and notes to volume 8 of the Hamburg edition of Goethe's works (it runs to 217 closely printed pages), opened up new territory.[4] Two years later Wilhelm Emrich's epoch-making study of the symbolism in the novel appeared, and in the same year Robert Hering's work was published, comparing it in a positive sense with *Faust*. In 1954 Arthur Henkel published his study of *Entsagung* (renunciation) in the novel, which concentrated on the philosophic content. In the same year Pierre-Paul Sagave, a perceptive French scholar, published two important articles, and another by Hans S. Reiss appeared.[5] Then two years later, in 1956, Schrimpf's book[6] and a valuable article by yet another French student, Claude David, were published.[7] As the latter remarks: "Jeder Kommentar der 'Wanderjahre' entdeckt neue Bedeutungen, und meistens mit Recht. Das Werk ist unausdeutbar." † Since that time important works have appeared at somewhat less frequent intervals. In 1961 Waidson's article appeared, in 1961 and 1962 the two by Friedrich Ohly. Nineteen hundred sixty-eight saw the appearance of what will surely be one of the definitive articles on form, that of Volker Neuhaus, followed the next year by Heidi Gidion's work, and in 1972 by that of Jane K. Brown.[8]

The study that follows is intended as a continuation of the work of the scholars referred to above. While considering the scientific structure, it will concentrate first on one basic question of form—that of the series of narrative insertions—and then of necessity on one matter of content that is linked so closely with them that the two are almost inseparable, namely the concept of the family as the *Urform* (archetype) and metamorphosis of the types of human association. To

---

* [His] energy is no longer sufficient to give definite and coherent form to a wide-ranging whole.

† Every commentary on the *Wanderjahre* discovers new meanings, and mostly rightly so. The work cannot be given a final interpretation.

concentrate on such themes primarily in a work of art as large and complex as the *Wanderjahre* might seem to run the risk of becoming a piecemeal, superficial, and hence partially false view of the novel, were it not for the broad and fundamental nature of such themes, which are present throughout the work in practically all its ramifications. Thus the intention is to contribute to the new and better understanding of the novel which is now emerging and which will, it is to be hoped, at long last help the work take its place as one of the two crowning masterpieces (along with *Faust II*) of Goethe's life.

I
THE PROBLEM OF FORM

THE MATTER OF FORM has always been the crucial one for the critics who have dealt with the *Wanderjahre*. The question is asked repeatedly: Is it a novel? It certainly does not seem to follow the traditional rules and models, which is all the more puzzling since Goethe had proved some twenty years earlier in 1809, with his *Wahlverwandtschaften* (Elective Affinities), that he was able to produce a brilliant novel of the more traditional sort, and although he does not identify the *Wanderjahre* on the title page as a novel, he does so later in the work (p. 118).

A valuable insight into the structure of this novel was contributed by Eduard Spranger in an article published in 1930, which, surprisingly, is otherwise on the whole negative: [1]

Der moderne Dichter hat . . . beliebig viele Welten vor sich. In der Regel wählt er eine—die künstlerisch beste. Er könnte aber auch außer der besten und fruchtbarsten eine Vielheit möglicher Weltperspektiven wählen, die die Ahnung aufblitzen läßt, daß die Unendlichkeit des Weltgehaltes nie von einer Seite her zu erschöpfen ist.*

A dozen years later he returned to the subject, dramatically modifying his earlier negatives.[2] He repeated his earlier idea that the work is "ein perspektivischer Roman" (a novel of perspectives), and detailed the complicated "counterpoint" that results from the use of four main perspectives in a kind of series. At first he listed the historical, under which he understands the Middle Ages ("St. Joseph II"), the eighteenth century (estate of Hersilie's uncle), and the nineteenth century (industrialism and the new world). Secondly he listed the ages of man—childhood (Wilhelm's tale of the drowned

---

* The modern novelist has . . . as many worlds as he wishes before him. Usually he chooses one—the best artistically. Besides the one best and most fruitful artistically, he could choose a multitude of possible world perspectives, which permits the idea to arise that the infinity of the world content can never be exhausted from one side.

Fischerknaben), adolescence in Felix, young manhood in Lenardo, Flavio, and others, middle age in "Der Mann von funfzig Jahren" (The Man Fifty Years Old), old age in the *Sammler* (Collector) and others. Thirdly, he noted the professions, having counted some twenty-five that were mentioned, and lastly, three circles of human endeavor—the socialistic weavers in the mountains, the league of *Auswanderer* (emigrants) and the group of those that will stay, Odoard's *Einwanderer*.

Jane Brown has dubbed this way of looking at the novel "multi-perspectivity" and shows how it is justified by a remark of Wilhelm's in the text itself.[3] She then goes on to demonstrate how widely this insight applies to the various parts of the novel. This is closely related to ideas that Goethe had about repeated mirror reflections, ideas that first came to him in his study of color phenomena[4] and which he later applied to life and literature in his 1823 essay, *Wiederholte Spiegelungen* (Repeated Reflections). Numerous other interpreters have used this insight, and we shall return to it. Obviously the elements that mirror each other together constitute a series.

Arthur Henkel passes over the question of external form as hopeless and seeks instead to find a unifying principle in an underlying philosophical idea, one that the author specifically includes in the subtitle of the work, *Entsagung* (renunciation). This concept is of course central, and it distinguishes the novel sharply from its predecessor, the *Lehrjahre (Apprentice Years)*. In the latter the emphasis had been on the many-sided, humanistic, "universal" education of the individual, a typical eighteenth-century ideal, while in the *Wanderjahre* Wilhelm renounces all that so as to be able to restrict himself to one profession, medicine. Henkel draws attention to numerous other aspects of *Entsagung*, calling it among other things the secular equivalent of medieval and monkish asceticism, for it is *Entsagung*, properly understood, which holds in check the *Dämonen* of power, of material possessions, and of sex.[5] He shows how Goethe applied this to individuals. The reader first made Jarno's acquaintance, for instance, in the *Lehrjahre*, where he was the wealthy and powerful natural son of a prince. In the *Wanderjahre* he has changed his name to Montan in honor of his new concentration on geology, and has fled human society for that of the rocks and mountains, apparently in reaction to the loss of aristocratic wealth, power, and position in the aftermath of the French Revolution: "Um nicht ein Timon zu werden, hatte er sich in die tiefsten Klüften der Erde versenkt" (p. 444).† Useful as the concept of *Entsagung* is in helping establish the unity of the work, Henkel is of course aware that it does not solve the question of form.

Goethe was well aware of the problem. He spoke of the novel as a "collection," a "complex," a *Geschlinge* (garland), *ein Straußkräntz* (a wreath of bouquets), he referred to its *disparaten Elemente* (dissimilar elements).[6] He called it "ein bedenkliches Unternehmen" (a delicate or hazardous undertaking): "ein wunderlich anziehendes Ganze" (a strangely attractive whole), "ein wunderliches Opus" (a strange work), and he frequently used the terms *wunderlich* (strange, odd), *sonderbar* (unusual), *merkwürdig* (remarkable), and *geheimnisvoll* (mysterious) in referring to it.[7] And to Eckerman he said:[8] "Es gehört dieses Werk übrigens zu den inkalkulabelsten Productionen, wozu mir fast selbst der Schlüssel fehlt." ‡

Claude David called the novel's structure an "open form," as did Manfred Karnick later,[9] although this vague and general term tells the inquiring reader little. More interesting is David's further comment: "Die Auflösung der Romanform, die die Schriftsteller der expressionistischen und nachexpressionistischen Zeit vorgenommen haben—man denke an Broch, an Musil—, finden wir bei Goethe noch viel radikaler durchgeführt."* Emrich agrees that the *Wanderjahre* foreshadows the form of the modern novel,[10] but it is really Hermann Broch who speaks with the most authoritative voice here:[11]

Und es ist jene Totalität des Daseins, die ihn [Goethe] zu ganz neuen Ausdrucksformen drängte, und die in den 'Wanderjahren' den Grundstein der neuen Dichtung, des neuen Romans, legte, aber es ist auch die ihr adäquate Totalität der Form, d.h. die völlige Beherrschung sämtlicher ästhetischer Ausdrucksmittel, untergeordnet der Universalität des Inhalts, wie sie in *Faust* alle Formen des Theatralischen sprengte.§

† In order not to become a misanthropist he had lowered himself into the deepest crevices of the earth.

‡ By the way, the work belongs to the most incalculable productions, to which I myself almost lack a key.

* The loosening of the novel form, which the writers of the expressionistic and post-impressionistic periods carried out—think for instance of Broch, of Musil—we find this carried through in Goethe's case much more radically.

§ And it is that totality of existence that pushed him [Goethe] to completely

Manfred Karnick tried to sum it up this way:[12]

So leisten Redaktorfiktion und Spiegelung in den Wanderjahren ein Doppeltes. Sie erlauben dem Autor seinen Gegenstand von den verschiedensten Blickwinkeln her zu bestimmen, und dabei doch als Geheimnis zu bewahren.‡

Then he concludes:

Und die Herausgeberrolle ist nicht, wie man gemeint hat, der notdürftige Behelf eines altgewordenen Poeten, der seiner Materialien nur noch unzulänglich Herr zu werden vermag, sondern ein besonnen gehandhabtes Instrument dieser Mitteilungsart: Maskenform in einer hochentwickelten Kunst des Indirekten mit "bedeutender" Funktion.*

The intention in the following pages is to make use of a method not previously employed on this work, to apply to the novel several patterns of thought Goethe had learned from his scientific endeavors. He said once that we write love-poetry as polytheists, do scientific research as pantheists, and deal with moral problems as monotheists (12.372). Still the pantheistic world view (he was an admirer of Spinoza) remained a matter of vital concern to him throughout his life. And for the true believer in God-in-nature, for the pantheist, of course, the study of nature (the natural sciences) is the true theology. So deep commitment to the natural sciences was always a part of Goethe's life.

His contemporaries raised the question as to why Goethe should want to use methods and techniques derived from his scientific research in his poetic works. The two areas of activity seemed quite separate to them. Goethe, however, was convinced that they were not. Summing up the gains of his Italian stay (1786–88), he wrote

---

new forms of expression, and which in the *Wanderjahre* laid the foundation stone of the new poetry, of the new novel, but it is also the totality of form adequate to it, that is to say the complete control of all the aesthetic means of expression, subordinated to the universality of the content, just as in *Faust* it burst asunder all the forms of the [traditional] theater.

‡ So the fiction of the editor and the [repeated] reflections in the *Wanderjahre* accomplish two things: they permit the author to define his object from the most varied points of view and at the same time to preserve it as a secret.

* And the role of the editor is not, as has been claimed, the poor expedient of the poet who has grown old, who is able to master his materials only in an inadequate fashion, but a thoughtfully manipulated instrument of this kind of communication; the masking form in a highly developed art of the indirect, with the function of "signifying."

in 1817: "Ferner glaubte ich der Natur abgemerkt zu haben, wie sie gesetzmäßig zu Werke gehe, um lebendiges Gebild, als Muster alles künstlichen, hervorzubringen."†[13] And he was driven almost to despair by friends who refused to see the connection that he, the pantheist, felt was obvious between art and science: ". . . nirgends wollte man zugeben, daß Wissenschaft und Poesie vereinbar sei."‡ He said that people thought that "Poesie und Wissenschaft erschienen als die größten Widersacher."*[14]

As an artist creating a fictional world in a novel, it was evident that he had to organize a large number of events, facts, and elements. Rather than do so according to the well-understood and somewhat artificial conventions of the traditional novel, Goethe, the believer in God-in-nature, was convinced that he could create a more realistic, a truer world by following the laws of nature as he understood them, in organizing his narrative.

The first of his favorite scientific concepts to be discussed will be that of the archetype (*Urform*, *Urphänomen*, or *Urbild*, in his language) and the various possible metamorphoses thereof. The poet found this pattern confirmed in his study of botany, where he had been observing the different organs of the simple annual plant—the leaves, petals, stamens, pistils, seeds, etc. The key insight came to him in Italy: "Alles ist Blatt" (everything is a leaf), meaning that the basic leaf structure is metamorphosed by the plant to fill each of the needed functions in sequence. The relationship to Plato's ideals is obvious, with, however, the fundamental difference that Goethe's concepts are always real, and, in botany, organic. He had a constitutional bias against abstract thought. In his botanical studies he identified and studied three kinds of metamorphosis, the regular or progressive, by which normal growth occurs, the irregular or regressive, which occurs when abnormalities set in, and the accidental, which results from the interference of outside forces. There will be need to return to this.[15]

The next concept to be examined is that of the family. When he

† Further I believed that I had learned by observing from nature how it works according to laws to produce living structures [which are] the models for everything artistic.

‡ . . . nowhere did anyone want to admit that science and poetry are compatible.

* poetry and art seemed [to be] the greatest adversaries.

turned his analytic gaze on human society, he saw the family as the archetype of human association, and noted the various metamorphoses of it.[16] Radbruch has a particularly good explanation of this (see below, p. 30).

The third concept is Goethe's use of the series. He early learned in his scientific work, while observing a confusing mass of phenomena, to arrange related ones in a series, proceeding by the smallest possible steps from one to the next. Thus a given animal bone could be most easily understood if put in such a series. In chapter 15 of this study there is greater detail on this matter. In this particular work of art the most obvious series is what seems at first like a number of novellas (this English term is a borrowing from Italian; since it is not yet really naturalized it will be alternated at random in what follows with the German *Novelle*). A closer look at the novel shows, however, that they are not all *Novellen*. Why not? Goethe could write as good a *Novelle* as anyone, as he frequently proved. In seeking an answer, or answers, to this question, the more general, even if vaguer, term *narrative insertion* will be used. These are numerous and important in this novel, and consequently much attention will need to be directed to them.

Two other products of his scientific thinking need to be mentioned, the concepts of polarity and what he called *Steigerung* (intensification or enhancement). Goethe observed the opposites of white and black, light and dark, wet and dry, etc., in operation in the natural world and recognized their key importance. For present purposes contrasts and differences will be widely noted, but the words polar or polarity used charily, as it is often unclear as to whether or not a given contrast is truly polar. Then in observing the step-by-step development of a plant, the poet was struck by the final burst of vitality that crowned a series—in the blossom, for instance—and called the final stage a *Steigerung*. Compared with the foregoing leaves, the blossom represents a higher and essentially different kind of development, and hence the special name. In this work of art such enhancements will be found to be relatively rare, but for that all the more important.

Goethe's use of scientific patterns in his poetic and creative works is a fascinating subject. It can be shown in his lyric poems and particularly in *Faust*, and most plainly in those things that he wrote

THE PROBLEM OF FORM 7

after about 1790.[17] For present purposes two examples should suffice. The 1809 novel *Wahlverwandschaften* (*Elective Affinities*) was based on the fact, discovered not too long before, that if two chemical compounds of the right sort, each consisting of two elements, are brought into contact, the chemicals may switch partners. In case contemporary readers should have been puzzled by the unfamiliar chemical language, Goethe had his "hero," Eduard, near the beginning of the novel, reduce the matter to an equation with letters: if compound AB is brought into contact with compound CD, they may instantly exchange and become compounds AD and BC (6.276). In the novel, of course, Goethe shows how this happens to two couples. It may seem radical and daring to equate inorganic chemicals with human flesh and blood, but Goethe did not think so. In an advance notice for his novel (originally planned as part of the *Wanderjahre*!), he wrote:

Es scheint, daß den Verfasser seine fortgesetzten physikalischen Arbeiten zu diesem seltsamen Titel veranlassten. Er mochte bemerkt haben, daß man in der Naturlehre sich sehr oft ethischer Gleichnisse bedient, um etwas von dem Kreise menschlichen Wissens weit Entferntes näher heranzubringen, und so hat er auch wohl in einem sittlichen Falle eine chemische Gleichnisrede zu ihrem geistigen Ursprunge zurückführen mögen, um so mehr, als doch überall nur *eine* Natur ist. [Italics Goethe's] †[18]

To compare a human being to a plant is naturally a much less radical step, and it is this that, in an outline to his autobiography, Goethe planned to do. In a preface to the third book, which he never used, he said:

Ehe ich diese nunmehr vorliegenden drei Bände zu schreiben anfing, dachte ich sie nach jenen Gesetzen zu bilden, wovon uns die Metamorphose der Pflanzen belehrt. In dem ersten sollte das Kind nach allen Seiten zarte Wurzeln treiben und nur wenig Keimblätter entwickeln. Im zweiten der Knabe mit lebhafterem Grün stufenweis mannigfaltiger gebildete Zweige treiben, und dieser belebte Stengel sollte nun im dritten Beete ähren- und

---

† It seems that his continued physical experiments caused the author [to use] this strange title. He may have noticed that in natural science one often used ethical similes in order to bring something closer which is far distant from the circle of human knowledge, and so he probably also wanted to trace back to its mental origin a chemical way of speaking, all the more so because after all everywhere there is only *one* nature.

rispenweis zur Blüte hineilen und den hoffnungsvollen Jüngling darstellen.‡ [19]

The use of the scientific principles outlined above—the three kinds of metamorphosis, the family, and the series—in organizing his novel *Die Wanderjahre*, is much less radical than either of the two examples just cited, and, as will become apparent, aids in making this work of art more realistic and believable. In considering the above scientific concepts, intellectual instruments, so to speak, it is evident that they are not only fairly simple and uncomplicated, but also that they are related, and even overlap. With these few tools, then, it is proposed to approach the *Wanderjahre* in the confidence that, since Goethe believed in and used them elsewhere, they doubtless play an important role here as well.

---

‡ Before I began to write the three volumes that now lie finished, I intended to form them according to the laws that the metamorphosis of plants informs us about. In the first the child was to sink tender roots in all directions and develop only a few seed-leaves. In the second the boy with livelier green [was to] develop step by step more differently formed twigs, and this enlivened stalk now in the third bed [should] hurry with ear and panicle into bloom and represent the hopeful youth.

II
THE NARRATIVE INSERTIONS

HOW ALL THIS APPLIES to the novellas or tales must still be determined, for this is the most obvious series in the novel. And, which is no surprise, there has been a good deal of attention devoted to these various insertions, for they are one of the most important features of the novel. Of those who dealt with the novellas solely or primarily, Gertrud Haupt was first in 1913. Then followed Emil Krüger in 1926, Deli Fischer-Hartmann in 1941, and Ernst Friedrich von Monroy in 1943.[1] In 1961 Waidson dealt with the tale of the *Fischerknaben* (*Fisherman's Boys*) alone, and Jane K. Brown analyzed all the novellas in 1971. And in addition, of course, practically all who have written on the *Wanderjahre* have had something to say about at least some of the insertions.

A closer look at the situation makes it clear that the first problem is the exact *number* of them! Korff counts eight *Novellen*, Spranger "about nine"![2] Henkel chooses not to deal with all the tales, restricting himself to "Die pilgernde Törin," ("The Foolish Woman on a Pilgrimage"), "Der Mann von funfzig Jahren" ("The Man Fifty Years Old") and "Die neue Melusine" ("The New Melusine"), after noting that some are "pure" inserts, some not.[3] Klingenberg also speaks of six "genuine" inserts,[4] the other, "non-genuine" ones being eliminated, apparently, because they were too closely connected to the main plot. Gregorovius had spoken of good and bad *Novellen*, classifying as good only "Der Mann von funfzig Jahren."[5] Then some critics count other elements as additional *Novellen*: Kunz thinks that "Die Pädagogische Provinz" and the Makarie elements should be so handled,[6] while both Peschken and Blackall claim the same for the portions centered around Lago Maggiore.[7] And Waidson makes a convincing case that the story of the *Fischerknaben* should also be so considered. Later in this investigation arguments will be advanced that the reports of Wilhelm's medical training are in a similar category. Altogether these form a considerable portion of the novel, as can be seen from the accompanying table:

Tales Goethe gave titles to	Page (in HA 8)
1. St. Joseph der Zweite	19
2. Die pilgernde Törin	13
3. Wer ist der Verräter?	29
4. Das nußbraune Mädchen	16
5. Der Mann von funfzig Jahren	58
6. Lenardos Tagebuch	14
7. Lenardos Tagebuch: Fortsetzung	22
8. Die gefährliche Wette	5
9. Nicht zu weit	9
total	185
Other, nontitled novella-like insertions	
1. *Montans Berggespräch I*	5
2. *Montans Berggespräch II*	6
3. Makarie I	14
4. Makarie II	17
5. *Die pädagogische Provinz I*	17
6. *Die pädagogische Provinz II*	15
7. Lago Maggiore	15
8. *Die Fischerknaben*	15
9. Wilhelm's medical education	12
10. Lenardo's *Wanderrede*	10
11. American Utopia	4
12. *Amtmann* and his labor force	2
total	122
Grand Total	307

Since there are 486 pages in this edition of the novel, the inserts amount to more than half of it; if one subtracts the two aphorism collections (a total of 52 pages), more than two-thirds of the whole.

There is another difficulty with these tales that is nearly as serious—how does one classify them? Goethe once defined a *Novelle* for Eckermann:[8] "eine sich ereignete, unerhörte Begebenheit," (an unheard of occurrence which happened), but if one examines only those tales given titles by Goethe, it is at once clear that he sometimes failed to follow his own definition. In the period before 1810, when he wrote most of these stories, he referred to them in his diary and elsewhere with varying terms: *Geschichte*, *Novelle*, *Erzählung*, *Märchen* (story, novella, tale, fairy-tale), but showed no clear preference for any one. The matter evidently bothered him, for when he came in 1820 to describe the period when he had been writing them, he wrote:

Hackerts Biographie ward vorgesucht, und weil ich einmal ins Erzählen gekommen war, *mehrere kleine Novellen, Geschichten, Romane* [sic], *wie man sie nennen will*, niedergeschrieben, deren Stoff mir längst schon erfreulich gewesen, die ich oft genug in guter Gesellschaft erzählt, und, nach endlicher Behandlung unter dem Titel "Wilhelm Meisters Wanderjahre" zu sammeln und zu vereinigen gedachte. [Italics added] *[9]

Then in the following year, in a *Zwischenrede* (intermediate comment) which he included in the 1821 version of the novel, but later dropped, he reported how he as editor had supposedly looked over the material still to be included in the novel:[10]

Ebenso begegnen wir kleinen Anekdoten ohne Zusammenhang, *schwer unter Rubriken zu bringen*, manche, genau besehen, nicht ganz unverfänglich. Hie und da treffen wir auf ausgebildetere Erzählungen, deren manche schon bekannt, dennoch hier notwendig einen Platz verlangen und zugleich Auflösung und Abschluß fordern. [Italics added] †

In other words, the above comments make it abundantly clear that Goethe had a broad and free concept of the form appropriate for these tales. He intended that they should cover a considerable range in

---

* Hackert's biography was sought out, and, because I had for once gotten into story telling, *several small novellas, stories, novels* [sic] were written, *however you want to call them*, the material for which had long given me pleasure, which I had often enough told in good company, and which after final treatment I intended to collect and unify under the title *Wilhelm Meisters Wanderjahre*.

† Likewise we find little anecdotes, without connection, *difficult to put under headings*, many, if looked at closely, not entirely simple. And here and there we find tales that are more carefully worked out, many of which are already known, (but which) still require a place here and at the same time demand a solution and a conclusion.

form from the short anecdote to the longer, carefully constructed *Novelle*. There will be occasion to return to this later.

A matter that has already been mentioned in passing is the question of the linkage of the respective tales to the main plot. Gregorovius refers simply to Goethe's Homeric "Hang zum Episodischen" (inclination to the episodic) and notes similar instances in the poet's earlier works.[11] Sarter comments on the number of instances in which Goethe provides no ending for the story concerned, but simply leaves it finally to be absorbed into the main action, providing thus for the transfer of the characters into the order of renunciation.[12] Hering quotes Schiller's figure of speech in referring to a series of *Novellen* as a system of planets circling around a sun, which in this case, Hering says, is the *Pädagogische Provinz*.[13] The reference makes an attractive picture, but since none of the stories depend on, or are even connected with the *Provinz*, it is of little help.

Ehrhard Bahr sees the *Novellen* as, to borrow the technical Latin terminology of rhetoric that he uses throughout, *exempla*,[14] that is, as examples of some trait or tendency from the main thread of action. To continue with the technical rhetorical language for a moment, he sees the mystery of the *Kästchen* (to which there will be reference later) as an example of Goethe's use of the principle of *obscuritas*. Concerning the *Novellen* Bahr is right, of course, as far as he goes, but there is more that needs to be said. Bahr is quite correct in looking on the *Wanderjahre* as an experimental novel, but that, of course, is of little help with the present problem of relating the parts to the whole.[15]

Klingenberg is more successful in the following assessment:[16] "Dennoch wird mit den "Wanderjahren" der klassische deutsche Entwicklungsroman auf eine neue, seine höchstmögliche Stufe geführt und zum Entwicklungsroman einer ganzen Gesellschaft erweitert." ‡ Insofar as the tales concern future members of the group that will emigrate, she is of course correct. But three of the *Novellen*, "St. Joseph II," "Die pilgernde Törin," and "Wer ist der Verräter?" have no such connection, and in two more, "Die gefährliche Wette" and "Die neue Melusine," the narrator plays such a minor role in the

---

‡ Still with the *Wanderjahre* the classic German novel of development has been brought to a new level, its highest possible level, and has been expanded into the novel of development of a whole society.

league of emigrants-to-be that he probably could not exert any formative influence on the league. Furthermore there are other more important members of the league about whose childhood or youth there is no explanatory tale, such as Montan, Hersilie, Friedrich, Angela, and the painter from the Lago Maggiore. And finally Goethe used a story to elucidate the past of a member who was not going to emigrate, Odoardo. More important non-emigrants, from the point of view of influencing the league, would be Hersilie's uncle and Makarie, about whom there is also no explanatory *Novelle*. So this analysis, too, interesting as it is, must be laid aside as having only partial validity.

There is another way of dealing with the tales and the main plot, namely, with cautious reserve. Henkel as early as 1952 warned against a too-detailed analysis of either portion of the work for fear of obscuring the manifold interconnections.[17] Kunz also urged caution because of the difficulty in separating the *Novelle* from the main plot in several key cases. Neuhaus too comes to the conclusion that a formal separation of the two is not possible.[18] In addition there is a stylistic feature which further obscures the distinction—Goethe's tendency to relate his story in pieces. In introducing "Der Mann von funfzig Jahren," he says: "Der Angewöhnung des werten Publikums zu schmeicheln, welches seit geraumer Zeit Gefallen findet, sich stückweise unterhalten zu lassen, gedachten wir erst, nachstehende Erzählung in mehreren Abteilungen vorzulegen" (p. 167).* Gidion draws attention to this, notes how it applies to the insertions and to the main plot and how it tends to make a neat division between the two more difficult.[19] Kunz figuratively throws up his hands:[20] "[Es ist] kaum mehr möglich diese Frage [der Novellenform] für die Wanderjahre einheitlich und summarisch zu beantworten."†

Finally both Gidion and Henkel note[21] that the main plot contains many elements that are reminiscent of *Novellen* and, according to the latter:[22] "Der Geist der ganzen Roman-Erzählung ist novellistisch." ‡ Neuhaus then draws the logical conclusion that it is only

---

* To please the habit of [our] esteemed public, which for some time now has taken pleasure in being entertained piecemeal, we first intended to present the following story in several parts.

† [It is] hardly possible any more to answer the question [of the form of the *Novellen*] uniformly and summarily for the *Journeyman Years*.

‡ The spirit of the entire novel-narrative is reminiscent of a *Novelle*.

the fiction that an editor has a series of story elements before him in manuscript to weave into a novel, the so-called "archive fiction," which is the unifying principle of the whole.

Whatever the difficulties with form may be, there is virtual unanimity among commentators that the content of the various elements needs to be dealt with comparatively, which in Goethe's language is the "Wiederholte Spiegelungen." Eugen Wolf[23] drew attention to a key comment from another work that includes a number of *Novellen*, *Die Unterhaltungen deutscher Ausgewanderten*. At hearing of the plan to tell a number of related stories, the baroness says:[24] "Ich liebe mir sehr Parallelgeschichten, eine deutet auf die andere hin und erklärt ihren Sinn besser als viele trockene Worte." * Trunz carries this further:[25] "Es herrscht das Aufbauprinzip des Zyklus, eines Bilderkreises. In ihm spiegelt ein Bild das andere wechselseitig." † He goes on to quote a part of one of Goethe's own outlines: "Dies alles gegeneinander zu arbeiten," ‡ and then the valuable letter to Iken of 1827:[26] "Da sich gar manches unserer Erfahrungen nicht rund aussprechen und direkt mitteilen läßt, so habe ich seit langem das Mittel gewählt, durch einander gegenüber gestellte und sich gleichsam in einander abspiegelnde Gebilde, den geheimen Sinn den Aufmerkenden zu offenbaren." §

Claude David sees the unity in the interrelationship of the elements: "Die Motive durchkreuzen einander und harmonieren in immer reicheren komplizierteren Akkorden. Jede Einzelheit erhält nur im Zusammenhang mit dem Ganzen ihren Sinn." ¶ [27] Korff sees the *Novellen* as core of the novel:[28]

Ihr [der *Wanderjahren*] Schwerpunkt liegt vielmehr einerseits in den acht mehr oder weniger selbstständigen Novellen, in denen wir einen Blick tun in die verschiedenen Formen von Herzenswirren, anderseits in den Ideal-

---

* I love parallel stories; one indicates another and explains its meaning better than many dry words.

† Here the construction principle of the cycle, of the circle of pictures, is dominant. In it one picture mutually reflects the other.

‡ To work all this, one thing against another.

§ Since many things in our experience are not roundly expressible or directly to be communicated, so I have for a long time now chosen the method of revealing the secret meaning to the attentive reader through structures which are placed opposite to each other and which, so to speak, mirror themselves in each other.

¶ The motifs cross each other and harmonize in ever richer, more complicated chords. Every detail gets its meaning only in connection with the whole.

THE NARRATIVE INSERTIONS 15

bildern menschlicher Gesellschaft, mit denen sich der Blick weitet in die wirtschaftlichen, sozialen und pädagogischen Probleme am Ausgang der Goethezeit.‡

As usual, one gets the best understanding from Goethe himself. After the novel had appeared he wrote to Boisserée: [29]

Dem einsichtigen Leser bleibt Ernst und Sorgfalt nicht verborgen, womit ich diesen zweyten Versuch, so disparate Elemente zu vereinigen, angefasst und durchgeführt, und ich muß mich glücklich schätzen wenn Ihnen ein so bedenkliches Unternehmen einigermaßen gelungen erscheint." *

Most significant of all was a comment that Goethe included in an early draft of the *Zwischenrede*, later suppressed. Here he addressed "den aufmerksamen Leser" (the attentive reader) on the number of separate elements already included in the novel or still to come: [30]

Der Nachdenkende wird, diese abgesonderten Einzelheiten betrachtend, gar wohl gewahr werden wo sie allenfalls hingehören, auch wird er in der Folge hiezu Gelegenheit finden, indem gemeint ist das Ausgesprochene sowohl vor- als rückwärts zu deuten, die Mannigfaltigkeit der Ansicht zu vermehren und die Reinheit der Aussicht zu verbreiten.†

Among other things it is significant that Goethe clearly had in mind two kinds of readers: "der aufmerksame Leser," "der Nachdenkende," (the attentive reader, the reflective one) on the one hand, and on the other the one who reads for the plot only, "Sollte jedoch der Leser, besonders das erste Mal, auf den ferneren Erfolg [Fortgang] der Fabel begierig sein...." § Such a one had a right to skip over to

‡ The center of gravity [of the *Wanderjahre*] lies rather on the one hand in the eight more or less independent tales in which we glimpse the different forms of complications of the heart, on the other hand in the ideal pictures of human society, with which the view widens out into the economic, social and pedagogical problems toward the end of the age of Goethe.

* The reader with insight will not miss the seriousness and care with which I have taken up and carried out this second attempt to unite such disparate elements, and I must consider myself lucky, if such a hazardous undertaking seems to you to have more or less succeeded.

† The reflective reader will, observing these separated elements, be very well aware of where they really belong, also in what is to follow he will find opportunity to do this, by which is meant to interpret that which is said forwards as well as backwards, to increase the manifold points of view and to broaden the clarity of the prospect.

§ However, if the reader, especially the first time, should be curious about the further development of the plot, ...

the next chapter. Here, then, as he had in a letter to Zelter years earlier, Goethe was making a distinction between the "gulping" reader and the "assimilating" reader, and writing primarily for the latter.[31]

It is on the highest authority, then (that of the author himself), that the "assimilating" reader is warned to be ready at all times to take any and all elements of this work of art and compare them not only *backwards* with preceding elements, but also *forwards* with elements yet to come. Hence in dealing with this particular novel, the normal, consecutive method will not suffice. In this study the consecutive outline will be followed in general, but the reader, who must be assumed to have the basic features of the novel already in mind, must be ready at any moment to look forward in the narrative, and to reflect on the significance of the contrasts and parallels that become evident.

III
THE FAMILY AS ARCHETYPE
AND METAMORPHOSIS

IT IS TIME to turn now to another principle of content mentioned earlier, Goethe's use of the family as an *Urform* or *Urbild* (archetype) and metamorphosis of the forms of human association. And this form, of course, is another type of series. The first step necessary is to return to the few positive voices that were raised in support of the *Wanderjahre* in the years before 1850, socialists all of them: Heinrich Gustav Hotho, Karl Grün, Friedrich Engels, Karl Rosenkrantz, Ferdinand Gregorovius and Alexander Jung.[1] The most important of these were the last three, who were also students of Hegel, from whom they derived their ideas about the family. In 1821 the philosopher had published his *Philosophie des Geistes und Rechtsphilosophie*, (*Philosophy of the Mind and Philosophy of Law*),[2] in which he stated, to begin with, that the first form that the moral substance assumes is the family. The family then "completes" or "perfects" itself in three ways: in marriage, in the material possessions of the family, and in the raising of children. Finally the family broadens or extends itself into a family of families, *das Volk*, the political façade of which is the state.

These ideas are very close to those that Goethe had been incorporating in his writing for years, with the difference that the poet conceived the idea-complex of the family as *Urform* and *Metamorphose*, that is to say in organic and scientific terms, rather than in abstract philosophical terms, for they were an outgrowth of his botanical studies.[3] These concepts can be documented in Goethe's work after 1790, and it is likely that Hegel's ideas dated from about 1806 at the earliest.

It is worthwhile to examine the contacts between the two more closely. In the five years, 1801–6, when Hegel was *Privatdozent* at

Jena, he was in frequent contact with Goethe. From the poet's diaries it is clear that Hegel called on him frequently and that they discussed philosophical matters (for instance, 10 October 1806). Goethe visited him in Jena, and he sometimes requested Hegel's assistance in reviewing books for the Jena paper (19 December 1803). After the military occupation and disruptions connected with the battle of Jena in 1806, Goethe inquired how various of his Jena friends had weathered the storm, including Hegel.

After Hegel's 1806 departure from Jena with his almost completed manuscript of *Phänomenologie des Geistes*, the two men maintained only occasional contact. Goethe would send Hegel copies of his newest works, and the latter would reciprocate in kind. In 1817 Hegel reacted positively to Goethe's ideas on color, which the poet gratefully acknowledged:

Fahren Sie fort, an meiner Art, die Naturgegenstände zu behandeln, kräftigen Teil zu nehmen, wie Sie bisher getan. Es ist hier die Rede nicht von einer durchzusetzenden Meinung, sondern von einer mitzuteilenden Methode, deren sich ein jeder, als eines Werkzeuges, nach seiner Art bedienen möge.*[4]

The matter under discussion was the *Urphänomen*, as Goethe made clear in a later letter:

Daß Sie mein Wollen und Leisten, wie es auch sei, so innig durchdringen und ihnen einen vollkommenen motovierten Beifall geben, ist mir zu grosser Ermunterung und Fördernis. . . . Da Sie so freundlich mit dem Urphänomen gebaren, ja mir selbst eine Verwandtschaft mit diesen dämonischen Wesen zuerkennen, so nehme ich mir die Freiheit, zunächst ein Paar dergleichen dem Philosophen vor die Tür zu bringen.†[5]

Although he was talking of the *Farbenlehre*, it should not be forgotten that he considered the family also as an *Urphänomen*, of course.

---

* Continue to take strong interest in my way of dealing with natural objects, as you have done up to now. There is here no talk of an opinion to be adopted, but rather of a method to be imparted which anyone may use in his own way, as if it were a tool.

† That you have so thoroughly penetrated my wishes and accomplishments, whatever they may be, and given them complete, well-motivated endorsement, is a great encouragement and assistance to me. . . . Since you act in such a friendly fashion with the archetype, even confer on me a relationship with these daemonic beings, so I shall soon allow myself to place a few of the same before the door of the philosopher.

THE FAMILY AS ARCHETYPE AND METAMORPHOSIS 19

In 1818, 1827 and 1829, partly through Zelter's good offices, Hegel again visited Goethe in Weimar, at which times their conversations were important, as Goethe later confirmed to Knebel:

Hegels Gegenwart war mir von grosser Bedeutung und Erquickung. . . . denn was bei gedruckten Mitteilungen eines solchen Mannes uns unklar und abstrus erscheint . . . das wird im lebendigen Gespräch alsobald unser Eigentum, weil wir gewahr werden, daß *wir in den Grundgedanken und Gesinnungen mit ihm übereinstimmen.* [Italics added] ‡ [6]

There is no external evidence of exchange of thought between the two on the subject of the family as *Urphänomen*, but the internal evidence in Goethe's works after about 1790, the internal evidence in Hegel's *Philosophie des Geistes und Rechtsphilosophie* (1821, foreshadowed by his *Phänomenologie des Geistes* of 1807), plus the contacts and correspondence outlined above, make it seem most likely that the two had indeed discussed the family in this way, possibly as early as 1801–6, more probably by 1818 and later. However, it seems idle to speculate on who influenced whom; the better course would be to stick to Goethe's own assessment of the situation, that the two had come naturally, and more or less independently, to an agreement "in den Grundgedanken und Gesinnungen." However, it is fortunate that the Hegelian system included these concepts, because they sensitized the Hegelian students Rosenkrantz and Gregorovius to the family problem, so that they were then able to recognize and appreciate the fundamental role of the family concept when they found it in Goethe's novel.

Rosenkrantz, a professor at Königsberg and a disciple of Hegel's, wrote a book on Goethe's works in which the family idea is mentioned more or less in passing.[7] His student, Gregorovius, however, then wrote a book on *Wilhelm Meister* that has become, as Hering noted, a minor classic.[8] Following Hegel's philosophical organization, Gregorovius starts with the concepts of the family and of marriage, noting the exemplary function, for the novel as a whole, of the *Novelle*, "St. Joseph II." He then describes how the concept of the family passes over into the system of education, where pedagogy

---

‡ Hegel's presence was of great importance and refreshment to me. . . . because what of the printed communications of such a man seems to us unclear and abstruse . . . this in living conversation we immediately make our own, because *we become aware that we agree with him in our basic thoughts and opinions.*

reconciles idealism and reality. Out of the family grows the *Volk*, which, due to the unity of blood, is a natural individual.[9] Naturally these are Hegel's philosophical concepts (he follows not only Hegel's organization, but even his language), not Goethe's organic ones. Nonetheless the insights are important. Only a few years later Alexander Jung expressed similar views this way:[10]

Die Menschheit als Gesellschaft, als die umfassendste Gemeinschaft auf unserem Planeten, hat aber ihren Grundtypus in der Familie. Die Familie ist schon das potenzierte Individuum, die erweiterte Persönlichkeit. Die Familie ist die Urassociation. Hier ist der Besitz zunächst natürlich.*

Klingenberg has then noted how some of Gregorovius's insights were lost sight of for decades.[11] The basic family-*Volk* idea, however, had to wait a century before Trunz[12] recalled it and restored it to its proper place of significance. It is strange that this idea should have been lost. Goethe of course was no socialist, so it is not surprising that the socialistic bias of Rosenkrantz, Gregorovius, and the others should have been ignored in the succeeding years. Yet in the process, apparently, many positive virtues of Gregorovius's work were also forgotten, among others the family concept.

It is important to note in this connection that Goethe had a high opinion of the *Volk* and of *Volkheit* (a word he invented, by the way); among the aphorisms from "Aus Makariens Archiv" is one on the subject (p. 470). To Eckermann he had defended himself against the accusation of not being a friend of the *Volk*.[13] Thomas Mann recognized this side of Goethe quite clearly.[14]

We need not even think of the warm-hearted scenes among the people in *Egmont* and *Faust*; we need only think of his personal feeling of well-being at folk occasions—for example the Rochus-Festival at Bingen—in order to realize to what extent he felt the folk atmosphere as a familiar, natural element, a nurturing valley of the subconscious and of rejuvenation. "Man cannot," he said, "abide only in the conscious realm; time and again he must take refuge in the subconscious, for there is where his roots are."

Henkel, of course, concentrated on *Entsagung*, from which point of view he recognized the important role of the family in assisting renunciation.[15]

* Humanity as a society, as the most inclusive community on our planet, has its basic type in the family. The family is the individual raised to a higher power, the expanded personality. The family is the original association. Here first of all ownership is natural.

THE FAMILY AS ARCHETYPE AND METAMORPHOSIS 21

Aber der Trieb ist schweifend, wenn er nicht auf Urbilder der Ordnungen bezogen ist. Eines ist die Familie. Mit sinnbildlicher Absicht läßt Goethe, die Welt der Wanderjahre öffnend, den Blick zuerst auf der "vorbildlichen" Ehe eines anderen Pflegevaters ruhen, der in der unangefochtenen Wiederholung des heiligen Urbilds seine Liebe verwirklicht.†

Peschken is impressed by the fact that Lenardo sees the family as depending on the possession of land (p. 384),[16] and finally Heidi Gidion emphasizes the way Goethe, in the fourteenth chapter of Book 3, as the novel ends, reports on the series of actual or impending marriages that take care of all members of our league of emigrants.[17] From this Gidion concludes that for the poet, marriage was a matter of supreme importance.

The family idea is of key importance for both the *Wilhelm Meister* novels. In this connection Trunz makes the following comment:[18]

Auch sonst liebt es Goethe, die gesunde Familie als Urform menschlichen Lebens darzustellen, sei es im Gedicht (Der Wanderer, Die glücklichen Gatten) oder als episches Bild (Sankt Joseph der Zweite). . . . Überall ist es die bürgerliche, neuzeitliche Familie, die nun zum Typus der Humanität wird.‡

Earlier in the *Lehrjahre* it will be recalled that Wilhelm formed family-like associations wherever he went; in fact, his living and being was within and as a part of family-like groups. As Anna von Hellersberg-Wendriner remarked:[19] "Erst der Eingegliederte ist der sittliche Mensch" (only the engaged human being is moral).

The *Wanderjahre* is the main object of concern in this study, however, and the central role of the family concept for this work can best be made clear with a few references from the text. At the beginning of the work, at the top of the mountains before entering the main flow of the plot of the novel, Wilhelm wrote Natalie words that betray an unclear and rather negative awareness of this aspect of his character and fate: "Ein Fehler, ein Unglück, ein Schicksal ist mir's nun einmal, daß sich, ehe ich mich's versehe, die Gesellschaft

---

† But natural instinct roams if not related to archetypes of order. One of these is the family. With symbolic intent Goethe causes attention to be directed, as he opens the world of the *Wanderjahre*, first to the "model" marriage of another foster-father, who in the undisputed repetition of the holy archetype makes his love a reality.

‡ In other connections also Goethe prefers to represent the healthy family as the archetype of human life, whether it be in a poem (The Wanderer, The Happy Couple) or as an epic picture (Saint Joseph the Second). . . . Everywhere it is the modern, middle-class family which now becomes the type for humanity.

um mich vermehrt, daß ich mir eine neue Bürde auflade, an der ich nachher zu tragen und zu schleppen habe" (p. 29).* A little later in the same area, Jarno, who in the *Lehrjahre* had boasted of his *Verstand* (intelligence, 7.433), inclined as he was to satiric and even sarcastic language, penetrated to the core of Wilhelm's being in the condensed and uncomplimentary way he referred to Wilhelm's future contacts with the people in the valleys below: "Wenn du nicht kuppeln und Schulden bezahlen kannst, so bist du unter ihnen nichts nütze" (p. 33).† The *kuppeln* (to play the procuror) refers to the founding of "families," (in the *Lehrjahre*) such as Wilhelm and Mariane, the Melinas, Wilhelm and Natalie, Wilhelm and Therese, and possibly also Lothario and Therese. The reference to debts recalls Wilhelm's payment of the obligations of the theatrical troop, which signified his support of a larger group or metamorphosis of the non-blood-related family.

Wilhelm became clearer about his main mission in life in the vicinity of and under the influence of Makarie. In his night soliloquy under the stars he came to the insight: "... meine Absicht ist, einen edlen Familienkreis in allen seinen Gliedern erwünscht verbunden herzustellen; der Weg ist bezeichnet. Ich soll erforschen, was edle Seelen auseinander hält, soll Hindernisse wegräumen, von welcher Art sie auch seien" (p. 119).‡ The concept of the family as *Urform* and *Metamorphose* is clearly expressed later, as, in connection with the story of the drowned boys, the reader learns that Wilhelm had inherited this way of looking on family and human society from his father. The father had worked to overcome resistance to protective inoculation against smallpox: "Mein Vater war jener Zeit einer der ersten, der seine Betrachtung, seine Sorge über die Familie, über die Stadt hinaus zu erstrecken durch einen allgemeinen, wohlwollenden Geist getrieben ward" (p. 278).§ The father's sense of responsibility

---

* It is an error, a misfortune of mine, my fate once and for all, that, before I'm aware of it, the group around me increases, so that I have to shoulder a new burden, one that I am forced later to carry and drag.

† If you cannot play the procuror and pay debts, you are worth nothing among them.

‡ ... it is my intention to produce a noble family circle, bound together as one would wish in all its members; the way is indicated. I am to find out what keeps noble souls apart, I am to remove the hindrances of whatever kind they may be.

§ My father was one of the first at that time who was driven by a general and beneficent spirit to extend his attention and his concern beyond the family, beyond the city.

then began with the family (*Urform*) and expanded to the larger metamorphoses, the city and the circles beyond. The fact that one is justified in using the concepts of *Urform* and *Metamorphose* in this connection is corroborated with the following language: "Er sah die bürgerliche Gesellschaft, welche Staatsform sie auch untergeordnet wäre, als einen Naturzustand an, der sein Gutes und sein Böses habe, seine gewöhnlichen Lebensläufe, abwechselnd reiche und kümmerliche Jahre" (p. 278).†

There have by now been several occasions to refer to the idea complex *Urform und Metamorphose*; earlier it was derived from Goethe's scientific studies. It is well to emphasize, however, that this same little tale, *Die Fischerknaben*, contains a most important statement:

Und wenn ich hier noch eine Betrachtung anknüpfe, so darf ich wohl bekennen: daß im Laufe des Lebens mir jenes erste Aufblühen der Außenwelt als die eigentliche Originalnatur vorkam, gegen die alles übrige, was uns nachher zu den Sinnen kommt, nur Kopien zu sein scheinen, die bei aller Annäherung an jenes doch des eigentlich ursprünglichen Geistes und Sinnes ermangeln. (p. 273)‡

If it can be assumed that this little tale is autobiographical, then Goethe is here confessing that his predilection for viewing reality under the two rubrics of *Urform und Metamorphose* is an inherent feature of his style, an important element in the essence of the poet's personality.

And yet, despite these partial insights into the problem, the all-pervasive and all-important role of the family as *Urform* and *Metamorphose* of the forms of human association in the *Wanderjahre* has never been studied adequately. It is the present intention to find out, among other things, what such a study will show about the novel.

---

† He considered middle-class society, whatever the form of state it was subjected to, as a natural condition which had its good side and its bad, its regular viccisitudes of life, good years and poverty-stricken ones in rotation.

‡ And if I may here add an observation, I must confess that in the course of life that first impression of the external world seemed to me to be the real original nature, against which everything else which impinges on our senses later seems to be only a copy which, no matter how it approaches the first, still lacks the original spirit and sense.

IV
"SAINT JOSEPH THE SECOND"

IN 1799 GOETHE wrote his friend Meyer asking what the pictures were that were usually used to represent the story of St. Joseph, husband of the Virgin Mary.[1] A look at the text of the beginning of the novel shows why: the headings "Die Flucht nach Aegypten," ("The Flight into Egypt"), "Sankt Joseph der Zweite," "Die Heimsuchung" ("The Visitation") and "Der Lilienstengel" ("The Lily") are used over appropriate parts of this, the first of the narrative insertions in the novel.

St. Joseph II recalls his life story for Wilhelm's benefit in the old monastic chapel that had originally been dedicated to the first St. Joseph, reminded by the frescoes of the similarity between the holy story and his imitation of it. But the match is something less than perfect. There was occasion to speak earlier of Goethe's propensity to make alterations in the received tradition; he is to be observed doing the same thing here. The biblical Joseph fled into Egypt with wife and newborn son; "our" St. Joseph has an infant and also two strapping sons, one by his wife's first husband, one his, and both approximately Felix's age (12–14). Goethe's family is not fleeing anywhere, it is returning home. And Goethe's "Saint" Joseph does nothing that would qualify him for the title of saint. In Luke's gospel it is Elizabeth who is very pregnant at "The Visitation." In Goethe's version Joseph II takes the highly pregnant Maria to his mother Elizabeth the mid-wife, where she bears her child. The final fresco shows even greater differences. In the iconography of the Virgin Mary, the lily is usually painted as a part of the annunciation scene to symbolize Mary's virginal purity, and is occasionally used to indicate Joseph's purity also. The traditional Catholic teaching is that Mary remained a virgin until her death, and that consequently she and Joseph lived together in celibate marriage, which the iconography indicates sometimes by making Joseph an old man with white hair and beard, sometimes with an associated lily. But Goethe's lily, the infant, is of course a product of his parents' love; Goethe's Maria has had three children, two of whom were fathered by Joseph.

On first acquaintance the reader is inclined to question whether this is really a *Novelle*, for it certainly does not follow the usual forms. Yet the author first printed these sketches together as a unit in the *Taschenbuch für Damen auf das Jahr 1810* (*Notebook for Ladies for the Year 1810*), and they have been referred to as a *Novelle* ever since. The purist is likely to have a further question about the title. The hero does nothing saintly, and so one wonders if just "Joseph II" wouldn't have been a better designation. But that, of course, might have caused confusion with an emperor of the Holy Roman Empire of the German Nation. Here too, however much accuracy might recommend a change, the designation is Goethe's. Schrimpf notes that the poet was not showing the man in his holiness, but in his humanness, and quotes a remark to Eckermann: "Ein religiöser Stoff kann indes gleichfalls ein guter Gegenstand für die Kunst sein, jedoch nur in dem Falle, wenn er allgemein menschlich ist."*[3]

There are further difficulties about the form. The three picture titles that have been mentioned ("St. Joseph the Second" is not really the title of a painting) had originally been given even greater importance in the 1821 version, where they were all at the same time chapter headings. In the final version only two are.

Riemann calls the tale a "magnificent" *Icherzählung* (first-person narrative),[4] yet it is one only in part. The portion starts with an omniscient narrator, shifts to Wilhelm's letter to Natalie, then back to the narrator. Only then does St. Joseph narrate in the first person, followed by another letter of Wilhelm's before final reversion to the omniscient narrator. Also, as Sarter points out, the tale is told in a technique which, since the coming of the cinema, has been widely termed flashback.[5] Gidion notes that the narration, which starts, stops for an interruption and then starts again, contains a considerable element of repetition.[6] Most critics in dealing with the content of this element of the whole have emphasized its ideal, exemplary role in all that is to follow in the novel. Here in the form also it is evident that the same is true: a complex insertion introduces a complex novel.

There has been occasion repeatedly to refer to the widely accepted

---

* A religious subject in the meantime can likewise be a good object for art, however, only if it is common to all humanity.

method of dealing with the novel by distinguishing between the main plot and the *Novellen*; here, at the very beginning, in the first insertion, it becomes apparent that there are frames within frames. Goethe uses the framing technique repeatedly in this novel, as will become evident, to set off elements within the conglomerate; there are at least three uses of the frame in "St. Joseph the Second." Gidion[7] draws attention to the way Wilhelm observed St. Joseph's family riding past so that they reminded him of the Flight into Egypt. The little procession overtook Wilhelm from behind some rocks, only to disappear almost at once behind another rock outcropping; in other words they were "framed" by the mountainous landscape (pp. 8–9). Secondly the report of the omniscient narrator frames the whole (pp. 7–11 and 30f), and thirdly, immediately within that frame two letters from Wilhelm to Natalie (pp. 11–13 and 28–30) frame St. Joseph's *Icherzählung*. However, to prevent the symmetry from becoming too perfect, there is one short segment of narration between Wilhelm's first letter and the opening of St. Joseph's report. And there is a fourth frame: Wilhelm descends from the heights to visit "Saint" Joseph, then at the end returns to the peaks to talk to Montan.

The time in which the *Novelle* is to be understood as taking place has been discussed in the literature; many have seen it as medieval,[8] but this can hardly be. The original monastery and associated buildings were indeed products of the medieval period, but they had long been deserted, had fallen into ruins, although some of the smaller ones were maintained by the representative (Joseph) of the present owner, a secular nobleman. Since Wilhelm speaks of the 1800 years since the original event, this tale is set in Goethe's own lifetime.

The place in which the action is supposed to take place has also been the subject of speculation. As Hering observes,[9] the mountain divide from which Wilhelm descends into "Saint" Joseph's valley seems to be alpine in character. The valley itself, however, seems to lie in only moderate hills, which reminds one of Thuringia's Paulinzella, a monastery ruins that Goethe did not visit, however, until 1817, although he had seen H. G. Kraus's colored engravings of the area before he wrote the insertion in 1807.[10] However, the actual model Goethe had in mind is not too important. Central Europe in those days had no lack of abandoned monastic institutions, particularly since the widespread secularizations of Emperor Joseph II of Austria in the late eighteenth century.

Much more important than the exact time or place are the paintings that served as inspiration or model for Goethe. There are two such series, the first probably that by the French artist Sebastien Bourdon (1616–71). As is well known, the *Augenmensch* (eye person) Goethe was deeply impressed by all types of visual art. He possessed a large collection of artistic and scientific nature which ran to perhaps 10,000 items, some 4,000 of which were reproductions of paintings, engravings of them, lithographs, or original drawings. He kept them in dozens of large portfolios, and for the last thirty and more years of his life one of his favorite recreations was to take out a portfolio and, with a small group of art-loving friends, go over each sheet with the pleasure and appreciation of a true connoisseur. Brown correctly draws attention[11] to a description of some of Bourdon's work that Goethe had published in his journal "Aus Kunst und Altertum" in 1818.[12] After Goethe's death one of his secretaries, Christian Schuchardt, made and published a catalogue of Goethe's collections,[13] which catalogue shows no less than seven copies of five different treatments of the Flight into Egypt theme by the same artist. The poet's description of 1818 probably applied to Schuchardt's number 21. The catalogue also reports "Flight into Egypt" paintings by Dürer and by a number of Italian masters, but the number of different treatments and copies, as well as the essay of 1818, make it fairly clear that Bourdon's versions were the poet's favorites. Bourdon had also done a "Visitation," of which Goethe possessed a copy. There were any number of painting reproductions in his collection that could have inspired the "Lilienstengel."

Both Gidion[14] and Brown further draw attention to the importance for the whole Joseph episode of several paintings by Jacob Ruysdael, particularly "Das Kloster" ("The Monastery"). Goethe had written a five-page essay on "Ruysdael as a Poet" in 1816[15] that includes a careful description of this picture, a copy of which, he says in the essay, he had before him as he wrote. However, the Schuchardt catalogue, although it lists reproductions of ten Ruysdael works, does *not* include "Das Kloster." There are several possible explanations: Goethe's copy could have been lost. Between his death in

Photo: Pfauder Jacob van Ruisdael: Das Kloster Staatliche Kunstsammlungen Dresden

1832 and the publication of the catalogue it could have been among the things his heirs sometimes gave away as souvenirs, or he could have been looking at a borrowed reproduction, or else he could have been drawing on his photographic memory for paintings and visual impressions in general. He had visited the Dresden gallery where the painting hung three times: in 1768, in 1790, and in 1813.

The importance of this painting is central, for it depicts a scene almost exactly like the one Goethe describes as the habitation of St. Joseph the Second: a former monastic settlement, the larger buildings falling into ruins, the smaller ones still occupied and in some sort of repair. There are several interesting aspects to this way in which Goethe drew inspiration from visual art. One of the most interesting is the parallels between the poet and his protagonist, who was also deeply influenced by visual art. Joseph had been named for the saint; as a child he had observed the frescoes of Joseph the carpenter, and had then followed the saint into that profession. The paintings then influenced not only his choice of a bride, but they actually helped him, we learn, in making the proposal of marriage (p. 27). In his words: ". . . das Gebäude hat eigentlich die Bewohner gemacht" (p. 15).†

Brown is concerned that the imitated paintings serve to undercut the reality of Joseph's world;[16] actually, this should be understood differently. There has been repeated occasion to refer to Goethe's concept of *Urform* and *Metamorphose*. What is evident is the result of a process to be seen elsewhere in the poet's works. With his intense love of and concentration on visual art, a favorite painting or representation would gradually come to assume for him the force of an *Urform*, and when he then later came to find something similar in real life, he would tend to see it as a metamorphosis of the painting in question.[17] It is evident that this way of grasping and reacting to the external world is almost Platonic.

There are a number of links between the main plot and the novella; in the "Flight into Egypt," the family is travelling, but will soon return. Likewise Wilhelm for the entire *Wanderjahre* must travel, but will eventually return (to the arms of Natalie). Joseph's marriage is ideal, his family is ideal, his profession, his relationship between art and life, his social position with respect to his contem-

† The building [meaning the frescoes] really made [its] inhabitants.

poraries, including superiors and inferiors, etc., all are to be considered ideal and exemplary for the experiences to follow. In addition von Monroy has pointed out some of the instances of *wiederholte Spiegelung* in this *Novelle*.[18] A holy model has been described in narrative and imitated in visual art in two parallel traditions, and on each side of this tradition the telling and the drawing or painting have been done an indeterminable number of times. "Saint" Joseph the Second, then, imitates the imitations, so to speak. And here Wilhelm plays the role of onlooker, almost as passive as he was at the beginning when he first observed the "Flight into Egypt" procession. It is also in a way a sad occasion for Wilhelm, for he is denied, at least for the present, what Joseph possesses—wife and settled domestic life.

Klingenberg points out that there is something a little ridiculous in the biblical reports on St. Joseph, a matter that was not overlooked in the iconography.[19] Yet Goethe makes no use whatever of irony here; everything is serious and idealized, the reason being, naturally, that he intends to portray an *Urbild* or archetype ("*Urfamilie*").[20] Radbruch expresses it clearly:

Sie [die heilige Familie] erscheint im Anfang der Wanderjahre als ein Urphänomen im Sinne Goethes, d.h. nicht etwa als ein geschichtliches Urbild, aber auch nicht als ein ideales Vorbild, noch weniger als ein typisches Durchschnittsbild, vielmehr als ein ideelles Strukturmodell, in dem alle die Eigenschaften vereinigt sind, die sich in der sozialen Wirklichkeit in mannigfachen Abartungen, Aufartungen, Entartungen entfalten. Hier ist Familie und Beruf, Glaube, Sitte und Arbeit, Handwerk und Kunst, Überlieferung und Gegenwart, Weltlichkeit und Heiligkeit in einem friedvollen Idyll verbunden.‡[21]

In examining all of these narrative insertions it will be necessary to use a standard technique and terminology: *external linkage* to the main plot; *parallels or contrasts* to the other *Novellen* or to the frame; literary *form*; *internal linkage* to the main plot; the *beginning* and the

‡ It [the holy family] appears at the beginning of the *Wanderjahre* as an archetype in Goethe's sense, that is to say, not as an historical, original picture, not either as an ideal example, even less as a typical average picture, but rather as an ideal structural model in which are united all of the characteristics which unfold in social reality in manifold variations, improvements, and deteriorations. Here are united family and profession, belief, morals and employment, handicraft and art, tradition and the present, worldliness and holiness, [united] in one peaceful idyll.

SAINT JOSEPH THE SECOND 31

ending; and finally the relationship of the characters to *sociopolitical superiors* and *inferiors*. Here the external linkage to the main plot is a natural one: Wilhelm and Felix run into the family group; they strike up an acquaintance and spend a little time with their new friends. To ask about parallelism or contrast in this series of sketches is to become aware that neither is the central factor here; this portion of the work instead constitutes an ideal, an example against which all the rest of the family groups in the novel are to be measured. Wilhelm himself was at least partially aware of this. When he wrote to Natalie after the first meeting with "Saint" Joseph, he referred to his plan to go ". . . zu einer wunderbaren Familie, zu einer heiligen Familie möchte ich wohl sagen" (p. 12).*

In form the account is quite loose. There is no attempt to arrange the elements chronologically; there is no trace of the dramatic aspect that is to be seen in the case of several of the *Novellen*. Nor is the account really a narrative; there is hardly any plot and there is no novellistic falcon in Boccaccio's sense. And the main plot constantly interrupts the insertion. With some of the insertions, as for instance "Die pilgernde Törin," the tale seems to be enclosed in a hermetically sealed compartment, off to one side of and without obvious connections to the main plot. Here in St. Joseph II one sees instead a series of sketches that depend on memory and association and which are loosely grouped under the titles of four of the many pictures of the holy family that were to be seen in the church. The beginnings and endings of some tales flow naturally out of and back into the main plot, and such is the case here.

The form then, is that of several reminiscent sketches, clustered about four visual representations of the holy family which attain unity when they are considered from a distance sufficient to allow a little perspective, which is also one way to view paintings. These opening pages are a model, then, in still another sense. Here on a small scale is anticipated what the novel as a whole repeats on a larger scale: a number of disparate elements, loosely related to one another (main plot, narrative insertions, letters, diaries, notebooks, etc.) acquire meaning if one steps back so as to place the entire complex in a unifying perspective.

The internal linkage to the main plot is, of course, the ideal of the

* . . . to a wonderful family, to a holy family I might almost say.

family. The poet chose the holy family not only to place the plot under the highest auspices, but for other reasons as well. To be noted first is that the ideal is the holy family *at an indefinite number of removes*. "Saint" Joseph II did not adopt the holy family directly as a model, responding rather to paintings of them. And the unknown painter of the frescoes stood, of course, at the end of a long tradition, a tradition that flowed through a religious and through an artistic branch. This is reflected in a sense in that Joseph not only cleaned and repaired the buildings (church and chapel), but also contributed to the decoration of them (carvings, stained glass); he had thus supported each side of the double tradition.

More important is the reason Joseph was chosen to play the central role in the ideal family. In marrying a widow with a child, he indicated clearly that certain types of motivation to form a family were of little or no importance to him: for instance, the egotistical desire to be the main man in the life of the beloved woman; for instance, the sensuous desire that drives many into marriage with hardly a thought of the inevitable responsibilities; for instance, the drive for social position, money, or power. Not only has Joseph II renounced egotistical gratifications, he has demonstrated a sturdy readiness to assume the burdens and cares of family life by agreeing to adopt a child he did not father. He makes thus a doubly ideal model for a novel in which the family as *Urform* and *Metamorphose* is to play a central role. Furthermore, he is considered separately from Mary and child, which is paralleled by the former ecclesiastical buildings. The church was dedicated to the mother and child, the chapel which had been restored and maintained by St. Joseph II, to the foster father.

The changes, additions and omissions Goethe makes in an original or model are of course invaluable indicators of his intentions. In response to the poet's request in 1799, Meyer had listed the paintings usually associated with the Joseph story, ending the list with two that Goethe ignored, the death of the saint and his apotheosis.[22] The changes Goethe made in the traditional iconography have already been noted: the number and age of Maria's children on the "Flight into Egypt," the woman who was pregnant at "The Visitation," and then the thoroughgoing changes he made in the portrayal and meaning of the "Lily." All of these taken together show one thing unmistakably: Goethe transformed the legendary material so as to fit Joseph as clearly as possible into the role of the ideal secular father of a family, and to make him and the family into *Urbilder*, archetypes, for the entire novel to come.

There is another factor which deserves constant attention in these insertions: the relationship between the hero and his social and political superiors on the one hand and his inferiors on the other. In Joseph's case nothing specific is said about his relation to the *weltlicher Fürst* (secular prince) whom he represents as *Schaffner*, as collector of tithes and taxes. It must have been satisfactory, however, for Joseph was well prepared. That the political area was well administered would seem to be the inference from the efficiency of the militia in the aftermath of the war (p. 22). And Joseph seems to have been on excellent terms with the common people. He refers to the superiority of the mountaineers over the lowlanders; his auxiliary occupation of transporting burdens would make him necessary and welcome among them, as would his mother's service to the community as midwife. Schrimpf notes this element in the work and called it "die religiöse Gemeinschaft der Tüchtigen"[23] (the religious community of capable people). There will be further references to this matter, but for the present, this much is clear: Joseph and his family are well integrated into the social milieu.

And so, having examined the first of the *Novellen* of the *Wanderjahre*, the truth of Goethe's comment already quoted is obvious—many, if "looked at closely, are not entirely simple.".

V
"DIE PILGERNDE TÖRIN"

THE SECOND NARRATIVE INSERTION, "The Foolish Woman on Pilgrimage," is clearly recognizable as a novella on the French-Italian model.[1] The heroine, a noblewoman, is wandering nameless and alone on the roads of France when she is found and invited to his estate by M. de Revanne. Both he and his son eventually fall in love with her and propose marriage. The "falcon" of the tale is her clever method of refusing both proposals by diplomatically misleading each into thinking that she is pregnant by the other. Hersilie had given the manuscript of the tale to Wilhelm to read before going to sleep, which forms the not-very-adroit external linkage to the main plot.[2] She reported that it was a translation from the French, and that she, Hersilie, felt a sense of kinship with the mysterious heroine.

The most surprising thing about the novella is that it is just what Hersilie said it was, a translation from the French. In 1789 a French-language periodical, *Cahiers de lecture* (*Notebooks for Reading*) (published in Gotha by H.A.O. Reichardt and apparently read only or primarily in Germany), printed the original, the anonymous novella "La folle en pèlerinage." It was quite popular in the Weimar circle, and Goethe translated it in 1807. Why should he have "borrowed" (not to say plagiarized) a fifteen-page piece of foreign literature by incorporating it into his own work? He could have turned out a better piece of original material; he had proved that repeatedly. In seeking an answer to this puzzling question it is well to note the poet's lifelong habit of incorporating extraneous elements into his work. *Werther* had contained a lengthy translated excerpt from Ossian; *Faust I* has a scene that follows closely parts of *Midsummer Night's Dream*; in *Faust II* he translates lyrics from *Hamlet*, and all except Ossian are used without attribution. In the *Lehrjahre* a whole book, "Die Bekenntnisse einer schönen Seele" ("Confessions of a Beautiful Soul") are probably the slightly reworked diaries of his pietistic friend Susanna von Klettenberg. In the *West-Östlicher Divan* (*Western-Eastern Divan*, a collection of lyrics), he incorporated some poems by his lover of the period, Marianne von Willemer, without giving the source. In his *Campagne in Frankreich* (*Campaign in France*) he had translated pages, without attribution, from the memoirs of the French general Dumouriez, and then copied the whole catalogue of a gem collection written by his friend Meyer. In all the cases cited there was a reason. And if he was intent on borrowing from French literature, why precisely this rather undistinguished sample? This is one of the central problems of the *Törin*, to which it will be necessary to return.

Why the heroine is on this particular "pilgrimage" is never explained clearly, but at the Revanne chateau one evening she sings a *Romanze* (ballad) that deeply affects her and that had made a deep impression on Goethe. He made a translation of it that was rather free in the first two stanzas (of ten) and which he published as "Der Müllerin Verrat" ("The Miller Girl's Betrayal")—again without attribution!—in Schiller's *Musenalmanach* 1799.[3] He then reworked it slightly for inclusion in the translated novella. With the tactful indirection characteristic of this insertion, the beautiful singer here hints at the explanation for her strange behaviour: her love had been untrue to her with the miller's daughter, had been discovered by the miller's family, had been shamed, and put to flight. The experience of being betrayed was traumatic for the *Törin*, for loyalty was one of her central characteristics: "Sie ist wahnsinnig vor Treue," (p. 62) and she says: "Männer und Frauen sind nur mit Willen ungetreu, und das möcht' ich dem Freunde von der Mühle beweisen, der mich vielleicht wieder sieht, wenn sein Herz rein genug sein wird, zu vermissen, was er verloren hat" (p. 64).* Trunz has summed up the situation admirably: "150 Jahre später hätte man aus diesem Stoff die Geschichte einer Seele gemacht, die durch ein 'Trauma' aus dem Gleichgewicht gebracht ist und in der nun

---

* Men and women are untrue only by intent; and I should like to prove that to the friend from the mill, who will perhaps see me again, if his heart will be pure enough to miss what he has lost.

eine Idee sich fixiert und verkrampft hat. Der psychologische Tiefblick ist auch in dieser Novelle" (p. 619).† Henkel also speaks of her "gefrorene Leidenschaft" (frozen passion).[4]

Klingenberg sees the tale as in a sense the central one of the novel (she eliminates "St. Joseph II" as being part of the main plot).[5] She further sees two groups of novellas here: first the *Törin*, "Wer ist der Verräter?" ("Who is the Betrayer?"), and "Der Mann von funfzig Jahren" ("The Man Fifty Years Old"), in all of which the love problems are finally solved; and then the other group—"Die neue Melusine" ("The New Melusina"), "Die gefährliche Wette" ("The Dangerous Wager") and "Nicht zu weit" ("Not Too Far")—in which group the conflict is not solved, but ends on a tragic note. One would agree that the *Novellen* fall into two groups, the first positive or optimistic on the whole, the second negative or pessimistic, but, as will become evident, there is reason to disagree with Klingenberg on the membership in the groups.

She finds three motifs predominant here: first the inconstant and untrue lover, which connects the tale to "Die neue Melusine" and to "Nicht zu weit"; second, the accidental meeting on the high road (!), which she sees as the link to "St. Joseph II," to "Melusine," and to the *Lehrjahre*, in which Natalie had found Wilhelm wounded and unconscious alongside the road; third, the rivalry of father and son for the hand of the same girl, which links it to "Der Mann von funfzig Jahren" and to the Wilhelm-Felix-Hersilie triangle of the main plot. Finally she claims that the similarities between the conflicts in the French tale and the other *Novellen* were what influenced Goethe to include this foreign body in his novel. Karnick thinks that what interested the poet was first the contrast between the purposeful travelling of the main characters in the *Wanderjahre* and the *Törin*'s random wandering, and secondly the sometimes puzzling half-revelations in which the story is told.[6]

In a sense the form of the material resembles the drama of analysis, for most of the plot is long since over. Her life after the reported

† One hundred and fifty years later this material would have been made into the story of a soul that had been pushed off balance by a "trauma" and in which soul now one idea has become fixed and rigid. This deep psychological insight also exists in this novella.

scene in the mill is really, as far as she is concerned, a petrified, psychologically wounded state without development; she is looking, with little prospect of success, for her lover. The result of his error is to condemn her to wander indefinitely, unchanging and unfulfilled. In the main plot and in the other narrative inserts, viz. "Wer ist der Verräter?" "Das nußbraune Mädchen," "Der Mann von funfzig Jahren," a journey leads to better understanding of self or of the circumstances, and brings resolution nearer. Not here, however: the vague goal of the wandering girl—to find the faithless lover—leads to no improvement and is nearly hopeless.

It at once is evident that the contrasts to other insertions are fundamental in this tale, particularly to the next, "Wer ist der Verräter?" This is Hersilie's tale, the next is Juliette's, and the sisters are very different. Furthermore, this tale concerns French noble circles, the next the German middle class. The heroine of this tale is presented after her fate has happened; there is no development, while in the next the hero's life unrolls before the reader as the action proceeds.

The question of family and national origins is, however, the central matter which forms at the same time as the internal linkages to the main plot. The heroine says "daß sie über Vaterland und Familie nicht befragt sein wolle" (p. 53).‡ Her experiences have "wounded" her (p. 57), and wounds, either physical or psychological, tend to isolate the sufferer. It is in this sense that she says, "Eltern hab' ich, und Bekannte genug; aber keine Freunde" (p. 52).*
And this is another area of contrast with the following tale: Lucidor's engagement was arranged between the families, and when changes became necessary, the families cooperated in modifying the original plan to bring about his marital happiness.

The role of the family in "Die pilgernde Törin" was apparently just the opposite. It is essentially this that Goethe has the heroine say to the elder Revanne in farewell: "Wer gegen alle Vernunft, gegen die Absichten, gegen die Pläne seiner Familie, zugunsten seiner Leidenschaften Entwürfe schmiedet, verdient die Früchte seiner Leidenschaft zu entbehren und der Achtung seiner Familie zu er-

‡ that she does not wish to be asked about her homeland or her family.
* Parents I have, and acquaintances enough, but no friends.

mangeln" (p. 63).† It is significant that in this portion the French original[7] is, if anything, even clearer than Goethe's translation. This throws light on one possible reason he included this translation of an undistinguished French tale in his novel; it made a point that fitted in well with his basic purpose in the collection of *Novellen*, namely that misunderstandings between the family and the loving couple could injure or prevent the establishment of the couple as the nucleus of a new family.

It is clear that the *Törin* is a negative example insofar as the family is concerned, and in sharp contrast, a polar contrast, to the ideal "St. Joseph II." The reason is the inconstancy and fickleness of the man. Now the French have long had a reputation (at least among the non-French!) of being notoriously free and lax in matters of love. Goethe could surely have written a better example of the bad effects of the proverbial French male inconstancy on the formation of a family, but what could be more diplomatic than to let the French condemn themselves, so to speak, by "borrowing" a French story, and an anonymous one at that, to illustrate his point! It should not be overlooked that the author had specifically called attention (p. 85) to the contrast between this story about aristocratic Frenchmen and the one about middle-class Germans (Lucidor's tale) to follow. One must concur that the author's decision to incorporate into his novel an entire French novella was in this instance quite appropriate.

---

† Whoever makes plans against all reason, against the intentions and plans of his family and in favor of his own passions, deserves to do without the fruits of his passion and to forfeit the respect of his family.

VI
"DAS NUSSBRAUNE MÄDCHEN"

THE NEXT INSERTION is really the first of three linked together (with "Lenardos Tagebuch I und II" ["Lenardo's Diary I and II"]) and the trilogy is from many points of view the most complex and problematical of the entire novel. Also it was for Goethe, apparently, one of the most important. During the course of the work, the author shows the reader something of the background of each of the more important members of the group of emigrants-to-be. Since Lenardo is to lead them, his history is of particular importance. And, as will be seen from analyzing "Wer ist der Verräter?," the development of the woman the hero chooses for a wife is also very important, because it takes two, of course, to make a family. In this case the heroine of the title, *Das nußbraune Mädchen*, or Nachodine, or Susanne, or *die Gute-Schöne* (the good and beautiful one), as she is variously known, and Lenardo, both show a relationship to their respective parental families which is crucial and unique. In "St. Joseph II" and in the tale of Lucidor and Lucinde the role of the parents in approving and assisting in the development of the marital plans of the son (daughter) was important. Conversely the *Törin* blames her troubles at least in part on her refusal to work with her parents. In the present case of Lenardo and his future wife Goethe is saying something radically new: the ideal marriage that will result is due in no small degree to the fact that each has reacted negatively against his family and parents. But this needs to be explained.

As the young nobleman Lenardo was about to embark on the traditional grand tour of Europe to cap off his education, his uncle, through his business manager, began to gather the necessary funds. Among other things he took the opportunity to get rid of an incompetent tenant who had been leasing some of his lands. The tenant's daughter, the nut-brown maid, a childhood playmate of Lenardo's, then begged the latter on bended knee to intercede with his uncle. Lenardo agreed to, but used inadequate half-measures and departed on his tour with a feeling of guilt toward the girl, which, during the course of his three-year absence, developed into care for her, and, as he realized only later, into love for her. She meanwhile was forced to leave her old home with her incompetent father, afoot with nothing but a few personal belongings. When then Lenardo again found her several years later, she had made herself into the able, respected, beloved (and well-to-do) key personage in a large community of spinners and weavers. The disapproval by the younger generation is implicit—Goethe never makes it explicit—but it is evident that Lenardo disapproved of his uncle's harsh and impersonal business judgment on the girl's father,[1] because he agreed to intercede for him. This, plus his guilt at having failed to have done so effectively, was the kernel of the emotion which grew into love for the girl. Goethe likewise tells us nothing specific of her feelings at being forced to leave her old home, but her reaction to her father's incompetence was to make herself into a skillful, successful, and well-liked business woman which, although neither yet realized it, is just what Lenardo needed in a wife. In each case the family has exerted a decisive influence on the rising generation, but in an unexpected and radically new way—negatively, as is appropriate for future emigrants.

The conception of the tale goes back to at least 1807, when Goethe's diary notes: "Einleitung der Geschichte der Inen in Briefform" (introduction of the story of the Inen [Valer*ine*, Nachod*ine*— the German preference for using final syllables as nicknames] in letter form).[2] In the fall of 1809 he noted: "die Novelle der Namenverwechslung" (the novella of the confusion in names).[3] By the spring of 1810[4] he was telling the story under its present title to acquaintances in Jena, which would indicate that at least the first part was essentially complete. It was finally published in 1816 in the *Taschenbuch für Damen*.

It is usually worth while to examine Goethe's names critically. "The nut-brown maid" is the title of an old English or Scottish ballad that Goethe knew from two sources.[5] The name Lenardo has been attributed to the French St. Leonard[6] and Nachodine to the Czech city of Nachod which is supposed to have been a textile center.[7] Finally the heroine's designation as *die Schöne-Gute* (the beautiful and good one) not only characterizes her, but is reminiscent of the Greek idea of *kalokagathia*. Horvath points out that during the period in which her religious feeling is strong, the moral adjective gets the emphasis of first position, *die Gute-Schöne*; after her religious fervor begins to wane, the aesthetic adjective comes first: *die Schöne-Gute*. And in this novel of many perspectives, the different names illuminate important aspects of the development of a very important woman.[8]

The question of external linkage is simple enough; Lenardo asks Wilhelm to undertake a search for a young woman, an old acquaintance, whom he fears he may have harmed but who, time has taught him, has made a lasting impression on his emotions. But the situation is more complex. The tale consists of three large parts, "Das nußbraune Mädchen," "Lenardos Tagebuch I," and "Lenardos Tagebuch II," which stretch out over much of the novel. As a matter of fact, in the outlines for the novel that have survived, Goethe referred to the tale at one point as: "Nußbraunes M 1,2,3."[9] Yet the change in title in parts two and three, to "Lenardos Tagebuch," is amply justified by the change in tone from the subjective attitudes in the first part to the more objective, scientific tone of the last two. In addition to this, the action of the tale is referred to in the main plot before the insert itself begins, between the various parts, and after the close of the last element. The next page shows this in schematic form. In the case of "St. Joseph II" it was appropriate to speak of the main plot intruding constantly upon the insertion; here by contrast it is proper to speak of the insertion interrupting the frame repeatedly. The beginning is not sharply defined, but is anticipated. The ending also lacks sharpness because of a postscript. And the gaps between the parts are strewn with material that has a bearing on the part to come. And so it is in order here to speak not only of external linkage between the insertion and the main plot, but also of linkage between parts of the insertion.

At the close of "Das nußbraune Mädchen" the link to the next part is provided by Wilhelm's acceptance of the task of locating Nachodine, so as to release Lenardo from the guilty memory. As the latter said: "Ich hoffe, wenn ich das Mädchen glücklich weiß, bin ich

Book	Chapter	Pages	Subject matter
I	6	72–78	Correspondence of Lenardo-Makarie and Juliette-Hersilie-Makarie, in which Lenardo inquires about Valerine.
I	10	127–28	Makarie asks Wilhelm to assist in the search for Valerine.
I	11	128–44	"Das nußbraune Mädchen"
I	12	148	*Sammler* advises Wilhelm on search for Nachodine.
II	6	225–26	Wilhelm finds Nachodine.
II	7	241–44	Lenardo to search the mountains for settlers for his estate.
III	4	336–38	Lenardo's interest in technical things, as introduction to following entry.
III	5	338–51	"Lenardos Tagebuch I"
III	9	383–92	Lenardo's great speech as *das Band*.
III	11	404–8	Plans for the new world.
III	13	414–15	One page introduction to following.
III	13	415–35	"Lenardos Tagebuch II"
III	14	446–48	Makarie has read entire *Tagebuch*, influences outcome. Final fates of *Gehilfe*, *Geschirrfasser*, Nachodine-Susanne, Lenardo.

sie los" (p. 144).* And at the end of "Lenardos Tagebuch I" the *Garnbote* (yarn messenger) provides the link to the next part by revealing the plan to visit Frau Susanne, the factor and economic focal point for the mountain weavers (p. 351f), and the center of "Lenardos Tagebuch II."

A view in perspective of the parts of the insertion, in a way similar to that used in contemplating the various elements of "St. Joseph II," shows that Goethe has here used the inserted material in a new way. In other instances, for example, "Die Pilgernde Törin," "Die gefährliche Wette," the tale existed as a foreign element, so to speak, enclosed within the main body of the novel. Here the inser-

---

* I hope that when I know the girl is happy, I'll be rid of her.

tion has been divided up into parts, with references backward and forward to the main plot, and the whole distributed through the three books of the novel in such a way that instead of detracting from its unity it actually aids in tying the novel together. When, then, one turns from the formal and external considerations to the internal actions, one sees that this effect is enhanced; the main plot flows into the insertion and the insertion back into the main plot repeatedly, and in ways that serve to bind the two together.

In further consideration of the internal linkage of the insertion into the main plot, the central role of the concept of the family as *Urform* and *Metamorphose* becomes apparent. "Das nußbraune Mädchen," with its introduction, is centrally concerned with the urge, the attraction that leads one individual to center his affections on a certain woman. Here it is, in Goethe's words, "Leidenschaft aus Gewissen," (passion as a matter of conscience) and he recognized that such was "[ein] selten[er] Fall" (a rare case, p. 448). The poet's use of the unconscious in bringing this out is skillful; Lenardo remembers the name incorrectly (Valerine, pp. 130 and 133), then shows evidence of the suppressed knowledge trying unsuccessfully to break through: "Wie ist mir denn . . . hieß sie auch wirklich Valerine? Ja doch . . ." (p. 130).† which betrays his feelings of guilt. Even more remarkable is his description of how a penetrating impression asserts itself: "Ein lebhafter Eindruck ist wie eine andere Wunde: man fühlt sie nicht indem man sie empfängt. Erst später fängt sie an zu schmerzen und zu eitern" (p. 133).‡ Notable is the wound simile:[10] we have spoken before of such things, and will again.

In this whole series of insertions Wilhelm's role is interesting. He undertook to help Lenardo find his girl for several reasons. First Makarie had asked him to (p. 127f). Then he is for the first time acting on the insight that he had received at Makarie's under the stars: ". . . meine Absicht ist, einen edlen Familienkreis in allen seinen Gliedern erwünscht verbunden herzustellen; der Weg ist bezeichnet. Ich soll erforschen, was edle Seelen auseinanderhält, soll Hindernisse wegräumen, von welcher Art sie auch seien" (p. 119).*

† How is that . . . was she really called Valerine? Yes, sure . . .
‡ A lively impression is like another wound: one doesn't feel it when getting it. Only later does it begin to hurt and to get infected.
* . . . it is my intention to produce a noble family circle bound together as one would wish in all its members; the way is indicated. I am to find out what keeps noble souls apart, I am to remove the hindrances of whatever kind they may be.

Thirdly Lenardo has asked Wilhelm to accompany him on his visit to Valerine, as "sittlich[er] Beistand" (moral support). In other words, Wilhelm is already beginning to function as "Seelenarzt," literally, "physician of the soul". But he already knows from Hersilie's letter to Makarie that the girl Lenardo remembers is not Valerine, that Lenardo has switched the names, but he does not inform Lenardo of his error. Furthermore, before they set off to visit the girl, Wilhelm emphatically assures him that the girl is happily married and well taken care of. Apparently he wanted to let Lenardo discover his own mistake. Such a conclusion is all the more likely in view of the fact that when Lenardo does discover he was wrong, Wilhelm skillfully helps him cover his confusion and invents a harmless excuse to conceal the real reason for their visit.

The question here is, had Wilhelm made a mistake? Von Monroy is of the opinion that Wilhelm did indeed err in taking Lenardo to see Valerine (the wrong girl).[11] But then, after leaving Valerine's, Wilhelm acceded to Lenardo's request to search out the real Nachodine, but demanded that Lenardo not attempt to see the girl, but to trust Wilhelm's word as to whether or not she was well off (p. 143). In the 1821 version the author had Lenardo tell Wilhelm outright that he had done the wrong thing.[12] Now if Wilhelm was right in letting Lenardo discover for himself his error about Valerine, he would then be wrong in attempting to decide for his friend about Nachodine. Using the terms of Wilhelm's vision of his future role that he had on Makarie's estate, instead of removing a hindrance from between loving souls, Wilhelm was adding one—himself.

"LENARDOS TAGEBUCH I"

This second part of the insertion series contains a detailed description in technical language of the spinning and weaving of the time. Goethe had always shown a preference in his poetry for figures of speech from weaving—"die älteste und herrlichste Kunst, die den Menschen eigentlich zuerst von Tieren unterscheidet" (p. 347).†
More important really is how Lenardo came into contact with these industrious Swiss. He arrived from the south, coming over the

† the oldest and noblest art, which really distinguishes men from animals.

DAS NUSSBRAUNE MÄDCHEN 45

highest ridge, travelling toward the north. On the way he followed a procession of pack horses bringing huge bags of crude cotton to the mountain weavers; in other words, he entered the landscape on the same route as their raw materials. His way on down the mountain then followed craft lines, the spinners higher up, the weavers in the middle valleys and Frau Susanne's establishment as factor in a town down near the lake. He underlined the relations of the parts to the whole by picturing the watercourses, small trickles and streamlets higher up, which run into larger and larger streams as the valleys open up until the large creeks empty into the lake. In other words, the human, social organization follows the natural geographical, geological features of the landscape. In all the houses where they stopped, the picture is that of a family happily at work in their own home, people who frequently sang hymns as they worked. By describing the social, economic, and religious sides of the life of these people, by depicting the watercourses and the connecting valleys, each with its industrious populace, Goethe is showing an integrated and articulated mountain *Volk*, the focal point of which is Susanne's establishment near the lake. Here, then, the family is to be seen as a unit and then through its various metamorphoses to its largest, the folk. As Lenardo said in his introduction to this part: "Dergleichen gibt jeder Vereinigung eine besondere Eigentümlichkeit; jeder Familie, einer kleinen, aus mehreren Familien bestehenden Völkerschaft den entschiedenen Charakter" (p. 337).‡

"LENARDOS TAGEBUCH II"

Here Lenardo finds his *nußbraunes Mädchen*, now called Susanne, and sees her as a member and leader of a series of family groups, from small to very large (*das Volk*). The name had been given her, in memory of their deceased daughter, by the parents of her fiancé before his death. Her role as center for the numerous families of spinners and weavers from the mountains is detailed, and her deep concern for them is reflected in her fear of the threat of the encroach-

‡ Such things [visiting among craftsmen] gives every assemblage a special individuality, gives to every family, to a small folk group consisting of several families, its definite character.

ing technology of the mechanical looms and what they will do to these mountain folk (p. 429). She and her unnamed fiancé had been members of the religious "family" of pietists in this area, a membership they had then gradually outgrown. And she related how she and her fiancé had been inspired by the nature poets of the time, Haller, Gessner, and Kleist, (p. 422) to a greater love for the beauties of their mountainous Swiss homeland. When Wilhelm had found her, the fiancé was of course still alive. Convinced that she was well cared for, Wilhelm had concealed her whereabouts from Lenardo, who was convinced that Wilhelm had erred in so doing, and who had now found her anyhow, her fiancé having since died.

Slowly Lenardo and die *Schöne-Gute* renew their old intimacy and come to an unspecified understanding—he loves her and she refuses another suitor for him. At this point her father, on his deathbed, gives them his blessing. Lenardo is to go on ahead to America. She will come later after an attempt, with Makarie's aid, to ameliorate the lot of the mountain weavers. At the old man's deathbed the two were joined by the assistant who had also wanted desperately to marry Susanne, but whom she had refused:"Peinlicher haben nicht leicht drei Menschen sich gegenübergestanden, alle zusammen in Furcht, sich einander zu verlieren" (p. 435).* Here the painful triangle of mutual love and devotion is a conscious contrast to the scene of triangular hatred and disgust which ended the tragic *Novelle* "Nicht zu weit" (p. 404).

The Lenardo-Nachodine love story was a matter of particular concern to the author from yet another point of view: this is the leading couple that is to found an exemplary family among the emigrants in America. Wilhelm and Natalie cannot function as an example in the *Wanderjahre*, as their love story took place in the *Lehrjahre*. Furthermore, in "Wer ist der Verräter?" the reader learns that the successful and proper marriage of the ruler has a significantly beneficial effect on the whole populace, something that under Lenardo and Susanne is to take place in the new world. Conversely, in "Die neue Melusine" and in "Nicht zu weit," negative examples of what can happen if the leading family is unsuccessful as a family are clearly depicted. Finally, and it bears repetition, Lenardo's attraction

---

* Three people haven't often stood opposite each other in greater pain, each fearing to lose the others.

to Nachodine is summarized as "Liebe aus Gewissen" (love as a matter of conscience).

In connection with the threat of industrialization, it is important to note that Goethe, as a responsible official of the little duchy of Saxe-Weimar, had long been aware of the suffering caused by commercial and industrial dislocations. As early as the 1780s he had seen the suffering of the unemployed stocking weavers in the neighboring Apolda. He had personally visited the home industry of the weavers in Switzerland on his trip there in 1800, and in the years following the Napoleonic era he had kept himself informed about the situation in France, as Sagave has shown.[13] Then he had followed a similar situation in Wuppertal in the late 1820s.[14] Thus it is interesting to see how Goethe was alert to an industrial development of tragic potential, a potential that was realized, unfortunately, in the open and armed revolt of the Silesian weavers years later in 1844, a revolt that Gerhardt Hauptmann was to make the basis of his shattering naturalistic drama, *Die Weber* (The Weavers).

There is still another relationship between the parts that is significant: the first part is predominantly subjective, the origin and development of Lenardo's attraction to Nachodine. The second part, "Lenardos Tagebuch I," is predominantly objective and concentrates on the economic and technical aspects of home industry in its simplest form. Part III, "Lenardos Tagebuch II," shows each of the two factors above on a higher level (*Steigerung*), and in addition shows them skillfully combined. Part I is subjective and psychological, while in Part III the history of the Nachodine-Lenardo attraction is raised to a more mature plane. It no longer shows the viewpoint of one person alone, but includes the emotional development of each of the two. On the other hand Part I deals with the family as *Urform* in a restricted and simple milieu; Part II shows the larger "family of families," interesting not only economically but sociologically also, that clustered about the factor Susanne. In "Das nußbraune Mädchen" Lenardo erred out of youthful inexperience and Nachodine suffered severe disappointment. Parts I and II of the *Tagebuch* show how each overcame his or her respective handicap and how they were finally reunited.

The literary forms used are well suited to this type of subject matter; in the subjective first part, and in the portions of the third part that concern the love affair, confessional, intimate conversation prevails, while in the technical and sociological passages of parts two and three the description is objective, dry, matter of fact, reminiscent of a scientific notebook, which is almost what Meyer's account (Goethe's source) was.[15]

But there is a new note here, the need to emigrate under the threat of the machine. In describing the way that the machine imperils the family textile handicrafts of the mountains, the author noted that some mountain people were actually considering installing machines "die Nahrung der Menge an sich zu reißen" (p. 430).† This ominous turn of phrase occurs again: "und wirst ihn [den Geschirrfasser] alle Nahrung an sich ziehen sehen." (p. 435),‡ which underscores the urgent emergency posed by mechanical looms.

When one turns now to questions of comparing and contrasting this insertion with others, one notes, as Trunz has pointed out,[16] that Lenardo, like St. Joseph, refrained from pleading his suit precipitously. In both tales a man was wooing an experienced woman, and in both tales the case was considered exemplary. In another way it is similar to the love between Wilhelm and Natalie; both couples were mature, kept passion in the background, and were deeply concerned with preparing themselves for a lasting and ideal union. And both couples looked forward to lengthy delays before their marriages could take place. In the "Das nußbraune Mädchen" complex there is a strong resemblance to "Wer ist der Verräter?" in that in both great care is taken to show how the loving couple is integrated into the larger social units in which they will function.

The great and paradigmatic importance of Lenardo's conduct toward his intended can hardly be in sharper contrast to the hero of "Die neue Melusine," the man who could neither control his passions for more than a short time, nor shoulder lasting responsibilities, nor practice any significant self-sacrifice. And climactic of course is the contrast between the Lenardo-Susanne relationship, which is an ideal, and the Odoard-Albertine relationship in "Nicht zu Weit," a tormenting tragedy.

The relationship of the characters to their social and political superiors and inferiors is also interesting. In the first part, "Das

---

† to snatch for themselves the people's livelihood.
‡ and you will see him [the repairman] seize all the livelihood for himself.

nußbraune Mädchen," Lenardo's father, a nobleman, and Nachodine's father were at odds, a situation which the son and daughter respectively tried unsuccessfully to reconcile, although the *Pachter* was clearly an incompetent. In the second and third parts the situation is much healthier. Lenardo, a nobleman and the ruler of an area, at the suggestion of the Abbé, went on a search through the mountain valleys for new settlers for his lands, initiating himself in the process into the life and work of the people. Susanne's feeling of responsibility for the common people is more strikingly exemplary. Of utmost importance is her outspoken indebtedness to the "treffliche vaterländische Dichter" (excellent patriotic poets, p. 422) who stimulated her sense of beauty of the landscape. So in the social ties upward and downward one can see a reflection of the course of the entire three-part tale: after a doubtful start the basis for a successful and even ideal arrangement is achieved.

There is yet another aspect in which the "Das nußbraune Mädchen" complex bears a close resemblance to "Der Mann von funfzig Jahren." In both cases Goethe took the rudiments of the tale that he had included in the 1821 version and lengthened it in a way that transformed it. Of the nine narrative insertions in the 1829 version, four were taken over with little change from the 1821 edition: "Sankt Joseph der Zweite," "Die pilgernde Törin," "Wer ist der Verräter?" and "Die neue Melusine." Two tales received lengthy additions that really transformed them: "Das nußbraune Mädchen" complex and "Der Mann von funfzig Jahren." Three of the nine are entirely new: "Die Fischerknaben," "Die gefährliche Wette" and "Nicht zu weit."

In one final way this complex of narrative insertions, itself a series, bears important resemblance to others: it depicts the course of personal development of the leader of the emigrating group, and so tells much that is important about the group and its goals. In the 1821 version Lenardo said (in connection with "Wer ist der Verräter?,") that this was one of the purposes of the collection of written accounts: "Da, nehmt hin und leset, unser Freund [Wilhelm] wird mehr Zutrauen als je zu Bund und Band fassen, wenn er abermals treffliche Glieder kennenlernt."*[17] In the final version the peda-

---

* Here, take them and read, our friend [Wilhelm] will gain more confidence than ever in the league and in the leader when he again gets acquainted with fine members.

gogical purpose of the exchange of biographies is described more broadly and explicitly: ". . . die Freunde gaben sich wechselseitig Rechenschaft von Gange des bisherigen Lebens, woraus ein Bildung entstanden war, die sie wechselseitig erstaunen machte, dergestalt, dass sie sich untereinander erst selbst wieder mußten kennen lernen" (p. 322).†

How great is the volume of material about earlier life or attitudes can be seen from the accompanying list of sources on the history of various characters from the main plot.

		(Pages HA 8)
Wilhelm	"Die Fischerknaben"; "Anatomische Studien"	24
Hersilie	"Pilgernde Törin"	13
Felix	"Pädagogische Provinz"	38
Lenardo and Nachodine-Susanne	"Das nußbraune Mädchen"; "Lenardos Tagebuch"	50
Christoph	"Gefährliche Wette"	5
Barbier	"Neue Melusine"	22
Flavio—Hilarie and Major—Schöne Witwe	"Der Mann von funfzig Jahren"	36
Odoard	"Nicht zu Weit"	11
	Total	199

In looking back over this insertion complex it is striking to note how Goethe has innovated in several ways. The use of the landscape and its watercourses to demonstrate the integration and filiation of the families of the mountain weavers and spinners into a *Volk* is most effective. Then too Goethe has taken a *Novelle*, *Das nußbraune Mädchen*, and not only expanded it into a three-part series, but has also connected each part with the others and with the main plot in a variety of ways. The negative stimulus that the action of parents can have on children is also new, as is the very important recognition of the suffering and privation which the impending industrial revolution will inflict on the handicraft workers. Finally it is worth recalling the criticism that in the *Wanderjahre* Wilhelm is no longer a

† . . . the friends mutually account to each other for the course of their lives up to now, from which a mutual education came which astonished them all, in such a fashion that they had to get acquainted with each other all over again.

proper novelistic hero, but a sort of travelling observer. Almost as if to justify this criticism, Goethe has so expanded the role of Lenardo that he seems ready to become the novel's second hero.

VII
"WER IST DER VERRÄTER?"

THE NEXT *Novelle*, "Who Is the Traitor?" is distinguished from the others in several ways. It was conceived in July of 1819 and written during the summer of 1820, more than a decade after most of the *Wanderjahre* tales.[1] It is different in another way—it is a comedy, with a hero beautifully suited for humor. Lucidor is just out of school, where he was a model student. He will become a model lawyer and *Oberamtmann* (chief official), and is a little stiff, introverted and pedantic, a perfect comic foil for a pert and snippy young lady, Julie, and her wild, harum-scarum brother, the *Junker*.[2]

The tale has not found universal favor with the critics, however, although Blackall calls it "humorous and sophisticated."[3] Riemann called it "eine gewiß nicht in guten Stunden entstandene Novelle" (a novella that certainly wasn't written during happy hours.)[4] Haupt says she cannot praise the story[5] and Brown calls it a fairy tale, a dream-wish.[6] Klingenberg dismisses it briefly,[7] and even Trunz called it "astonishingly light-weight," saying that it could not count as a peak performance on the *Novelle*, but as a valley, full of everyday, unimportant things.[8] Von Monroy thought the joke involved "second rate."[9]

Despite all this the tale is exemplary in yet another fashion: as Goethe recounts the various hindrances that strew the path of true love and the different solutions that lead slowly to a happy consummation, he takes the opportunity to indicate unmistakably the qualities that fit an individual to enter into a good family relationship, as well as the desirable preparatory processes. This will be demonstrated.

Our hero, Lucidor, son of a professor, has been promised in childhood to the daughter of a befriended *Oberamtmann*, whom, after a period of apprenticeship, he is to succeed. Having just finished school, he arrives for a visit to renew his acquaintance with his promised Julie. Imagine his chagrin to find that he cannot stand her, but is instead deeply smitten by her younger sister Lucinde. Due to his introverted nature he finds it hard to communicate (Goethe is here satirizing the typical bookish lawyer), but at night after retiring to his room, he holds, aloud, an impassioned monologue on the events of the day and plans next day to speak to the girl's father. Unbeknownst to him, his hosts have overheard his monologue. They are all, including the two young ladies, perfectly agreeable to Lucidor's shift in affections, but want the approval of his father, who is away on a trip. So they play for time, and next morning Lucidor finds that the girls' father he wanted to speak to had been suddenly "called away." That night in his monologue, Lucidor resolved to speak to an older friend of the family, only to find next day that he too is unavailable. This goes on for four days. Finally he decides to leave this frustrating house, only to find next day that the wild *Junker* brother, without so much as a by-your-leave, has ridden off on his horse! Of course, as is proper in light comedy, boy eventually gets girl and all live happily ever after. In the final scene, Julie takes Lucidor for a carriage ride through the countryside which he will in the future govern and explains everything in dramatic form, even including stage directions. In other words, the monologues end with a dialogue.

The external linkage to the main plot is similar to that of the *Törin*, and similarly superficial. The tale is sent to Wilhelm by Juliette, Hersilie's sister. This is all the more interesting since as Hersilie resembled the heroine of "Die pilgernde Törin," Juliette resembled Lucinde. Her practical and matter-of-fact uncle had nothing but praise for Juliette: ". . . sie ist ein wackeres Mädchen, das noch etwas lernen und begreifen mag" (p. 70).* She did not, like Hersilie, compare herself with the heroine of her tale, but it is impossible not to notice the similarity between the pairs of sisters: Julie resembling Hersilie "neckisch, lieblich, unstät, höchst unterhaltend" (teasing, lovely, restless, very entertaining, p. 87), and Lucinde resembling Juliette, "die andere zu bezeichnen schwer, weil sie in Geradheit und Reinheit dasjenige darstellte, was wir an allen Frauen wünschenswert finden" (p. 87).† The external linkage seems, then, to be quite superficial, but actually it reflects a good

---
* . . . she is a fine girl that still wants to learn and understand things.

† the other hard to describe, because she represented in straightness and purity that which we find desirable in all women.

deal about Juliette. To be noted here as in the case of "Die pilgernde Törin" is that in the 1821 version the tale was simply read by Friedrich to Wilhelm from Lenardo's collection of documents,[10] with the general comment: "Jedes Blatt in Lenardos Archiv ist im Sinne des Ganzen, und wie er mir diese gab, so sagte er: 'Da, nehmt hin und leset; unser Freund wird mehr Zutrauen als je zu Bund und Band fassen, wenn er abermals treffliche Glieder kennen lernt.'" ‡[11] Again this tale does not flow out of or back into the main plot (note the beginning and ending); it seems to exist in a sealed compartment.

The question of contrast and parallels to the other elements in the novel has already been touched on: this is the German middle class, the *Törin* dealt with the French aristocracy; this ends happily in two engagements, that is tragic; this owes the successful resolution to the intelligent activities of the two families, while the French ended in renunciation for which the misunderstanding of the family was apparently largely responsible; the hero and heroine here are closely identified with the family and with one of the larger metamorphoses thereof, the common people, while the French heroine had cut herself off from both.

An interesting corroboration of the close relationship that Goethe conceived between "Die pilgernde Törin" and "Wer ist der Verräter?" is to be seen from his surviving outlines. In the 1821 version the two tales had come close together toward the end of the novel. In the first outline that he drew up after he decided to rewrite the novel, apparently from the end of June 1825,[12] he moved the "Törin" forward into the early part of the novel, leaving the other in its original end position. In a subsequent revision of this outline, undated, the "Verräter" was moved forward to a position shortly after the "Törin," but the poet forgot to cross it out at the end. It would seem then that after some wavering, the author confirmed his original judgment that the two should appear together, doubtless for purposes of comparison and contrast.

There are other similarities and differences that range farther

---

‡ Every page in Lenardo's archive is in line with the main ideas, and as he gave me these he said: "Here, take them and read; our friend [Wilhelm] will gain more confidence than ever in the league and in the leader, when he again gets acquainted with fine members."

afield. In the sense that the tale portrays a couple overcoming the difficulties that keep them apart, there is some resemblance to "Der Mann von funfzig Jahren." In the sense that it ends happily, it contrasts with the most tragic of all, "Nicht zu weit." Of all the narrative insertions in the novel, this is the only one, aside from the ideal "St. Joseph II," that ends within the tale itself in a happy and successful love affair, which means the foundation of a new family. To be sure "Das nußbraune Mädchen," and "Der Mann von funfzig Jahren" eventually are concluded successfully, but presumably only after the ending of the main plot. In a contrasting fashion there are two insertions in which the attempt to form a family ends unsuccessfully: the failure of "Die neue Melusine" and the deep tragedy of "Nicht zu weit." In a real sense, then, "Wer ist der Verräter?" is a model of the happy and successful resolution of the problems involved in founding a family, and as such deserves comparison with the ideal pictures that opened the novel in "Sankt Joseph der Zweite."

The form is further interesting in that there is a repetitive motion to the plot which is made to order for a romantic comedy. The "falcon," the overheard monologues, occurs five times (pp. 86, 91, 92, 96, and 99). Likewise the hero takes five excursions or trips away from the house of his host, the last two of which look like flights. They are: 1) the trip to view the *Anlagen* and the *Triftraum* (plantings and fair grounds) on the return (pp. 93f); 2) the hunt (p. 97); 3) the trip on foot after his horse had been "borrowed," to see his university friend (intercepted by the old gentleman, p. 101); 4) his flight from the crowded salon (p. 106, intercepted this time by Lucinde before the mirror); and 5) the carriage excursion through the already familiar areas with Julie, during which all is explained.

Another repetitive reference here is to the mirror in the *Gartensaal* (garden room). There have been several references to Goethe's use of "wiederholte Spiegelungen." His practice in this instance is particularly illuminating. On the first (of four) occasions on which it is mentioned (p. 94) its role is compared to that of art. By looking from the actual scene to the reflection (mirror or art), one's attraction to both is heightened.[13] On the second occasion of its mention the mirror is a threatening force. It reflects the sun, dazzling Lucidor and causing the introvert to retire into himself; he has received an emotional wound, for below the mirror the Italian visitor Antoni is kissing the hand of his beloved Lucinde. At her insistence he then seats himself on the sofa (p. 99), forming thus a momentary triangle picture which sums up this part of his mistakes about Lucinde, as do similar triangle pictures in "Der Mann von funfzig Jahren" (p. 214), "Nicht zu weit" (p. 404), and "Lenardos Tagebuch II" (p. 434). The third time that he notes the mirror it is to see himself happily kissing Lucinde, and again the mirror and the reality enhance each other. Both of the last two references have been deeply colored by the subjective state of the beholder, Lucidor. The fourth and last time the mirror is mentioned Julie refers to it on their drive of explanation (p. 110) in a way that returns the mirror to its impersonal function.

The matter of education forms an important note in this *Novelle*, foreshadowing the role it is to play in the novel. The *Lehrjahre* represent Wilhelm's education, or at least the conclusion of it; in the *Wanderjahre* Wilhelm is deeply concerned with Felix's education (Pädagogische Provinz) and with his own medical studies. There was also reference to the development (art and apprenticeship) of Joseph. We shall see how, in "Der Mann von funfzig Jahren," education in classical literature plays a role for the Major, while training in modern literature does the same for his son Flavio. It is meaningful here that Lucidor's education is outlined (pp. 87–89) with clear indication not only of his success at school, but also of that education's appropriateness to the position he was to occupy in life. Likewise Julie's "education" (geography and topology) is noted as appropriate, since it involved politics and commerce, for the supposed future wife of a future *Amtmann* (p. 87).

Finally the relationship of the hero to the ruler of the land and to the common people is important for an *Oberamtmann*. They lived "in einem glücklichen Fürstenlande" (in a happy principality, p. 86), which assured tenure to a man of ability, and the plan to have Lucidor succeed the *Oberamtmann* had family and governmental approval (p. 87). The happy relationship to the common people is indicated most clearly by the first excursion that they took. On the way out the party inspected the park and the plantings, the pleasure and avocation of the wealthy (pp. 93–94), but on the return they made a detour to the amusement park (*Triftraum*, p. 95) which had been erected at the instigation of the younger brother for the amusement of the common people. This care for the welfare and recreation of the common people is emphasized in Julie's carriage ride with Lucidor. She drew his attention to "die hübschen Bauersleute" (the handsome peasants, p. 109), and then took him to a hilltop: ". . . ich will Ihnen die Reiche der Welt und ihre Herrlichkeit zeigen. . . . Wie klar das ebene Land gegen das Gebirg hinliegt. Alle diese Dörfer verdanken meinem Vater gar viel, und Mutter und Töchter wohl auch. Die Flur jenes Städtchens dort hinten macht erst die Grenze" (p. 109).* Thus Lucidor got an overview of the land he is to administer. She then noted the closer view. They passed the amusement park on the return, at which the people showed their goodwill and affection by greeting them with: "O das schöne Paar!" (oh, the lovely couple!, p. 113).

Lucidor had been drawn to an old gentleman, friend of the family, who had a collection of portraits of patriotic and political heroes, whom he extolled as ideals (p. 101f). Thus it becomes clear that in this model *Novelle* Goethe is saying that the model family should be integrated successfully into the immediate community and into the larger political entity, and should possess a sense of historical continuity as well.

---

* . . . I intend to show you the realms of the world and their magnificence. . . . How clearly the plain borders against the mountains there. All these villages owe much to my father, and to mother and daughters probably also. Not until you get to the lands of that little city over there do you get to the border.

VIII
"DER MANN VON FUNFZIG JAHREN"

THE NEXT NOVELLA, "The Man Fifty Years Old," is the longest of all,[1] and in its external linkage it is also unique. It is the only one without even a superficial connection to the main plot at the beginning; the author merely assures the reader that by the *end* the relationship will have become obvious (p. 117). In the 1821 version the internal linkage was quite different; there one finds only the first third of the *Novelle*, and that is introduced as an enclosure in a letter from Hersilie to Wilhelm. And that first third ended with the prospect of the Major marrying Hilarie, Flavio the beautiful widow, which makes a completely different impression from the final version. But, as Trunz points out (p. 667), there are hints even in this truncated beginning that lead one to expect a further development that does not occur. And then, too, the 1821 version contains in Hilarie's letter a reference to two travelling ladies,[2] who, in view of the 1829 version, can only be Hilarie and the beautiful widow on their way to or at Lago Maggiore—but there is no explanation for this in the 1821 version. In other words, the full *Novelle* probably existed, at least in plan, by 1821.

Goethe worked on this tale longer than on any other part of the novel (from 1803 to 1827), some twenty-four years,[3] from which it is apparent that the problems it contained were of particular interest to the poet—of which more presently.

No less than eleven outlines for this *Novelle* have survived,[4] only one of which dates from before the publication of the 1821 version (13 November 1820). But from that one it is obvious that Goethe already had in mind the complete action of the eventual form of the *Novelle*. The necessary inference is that in 1821 he planned a later continuation of the novel, in which the final portions of this, as well as of "Das nußbraune Mädchen," would appear. This would seem to be borne out by the fact that the title page of the 1821 edition carried the note "erster Teil," without any second part being indicated. And he mentioned a planned *Meisterjahre* to Kanzler Muller in 1821.[5] It was noted above how the distribution of the parts of "Das nußbraune Mädchen" throughout the novel tended to tie the whole together. It would seem that Goethe's intention in 1821 was to use "Der Mann von funfzig Jahren" in this way also.

The connection to the main plot at the end is explicit, but the ending is a ragged one, in that no final conclusion on the fate of the characters is reached within the *Novelle* itself. The reader learns only later from postscripts (pp. 226f, 437) what the final solution was. In form the material is dramatic; one of the outlines, as a matter of fact, divides the material into acts and scenes.[6] In addition, there are two plots which are linked, and yet each reaches its climax at different times (Major-Hilarie, chapter 4; Flavio-widow, chapter 5). This staggering of the plots is paralleled also in the discrepancy between external and internal events: both serve as sources of dramatic tension. "Die Empfindung scheint der Situation meist vorauszueilen oder hinter ihr zurückzubleiben, . . . identisch sind sie so gut wie nie."*[7]

The internal linkage concerns the family, but it remains, so to speak, within the family. Here Goethe is concentrating on two problems: first, settling the financial and property division between the members of this one wealthy and aristocratic family, and secondly, correcting the love affairs that are crossed between generations, i.e., the older Major is in love with his niece Hilarie, and his son Flavio is in love with the older "schöne Witwe" (beautiful widow). In "Lenardos Tagebuch I und II" close attention was devoted to the larger economic, social, and religious metamorphoses of the family. As will be seen, there is some of that in this insertion, but the emphasis is on this one family. It should not be overlooked that this insertion comes early in Book II of the novel, "Lenardos Tagebuch I und II" in the middle and at the end of Book III. In other words, Goethe introduces the reader first to the simple family as *Urform* (St. Joseph II), and only gradually to the larger metamorphoses thereof.

The sense of family unity is very strong as the action commences,

---

* The feeling seems mostly to either hurry ahead of the situation or lag behind it, . . . they are almost never identical.

but it is a feeling that is questionable insofar as it places too much emphasis on questions of property. The original plan of marrying Flavio and Hilarie was based in large part on considerations of the family holdings. When the Major then heard that the girl's affections were engaged elsewhere (before learning that they concerned himself), he burst out: ". . . indessen wir uns alle Mühe geben, uns ökonomisch vorzusehen, so spielt uns die Neigung einen solchen Streich" (p. 168).† The irony of this is increased when, on learning that he is the object of the affections of his niece, he stated "daß Neigungen dieser Art nur scheinbar sind, daß ein Selbstbetrug dahinter verborgen liegt" (p. 169).‡ And then he called the attraction unnatural! The Major's mental obtuseness should not be overlooked here. The ironic note is everywhere in these opening pages. In making such shortsighted remarks the Major is being cast, of course, in the role of the comic parent, traditional in light comedy, which is the form in which Goethe first conceived the novella. However, there will be reason to take further note of the Major's density.

How important a role the matters of family possessions played in an eventual union of the Major and Hilarie is reflected in the frequency with which they are mentioned: pp. 168, 169, 179, 181, 183, 194–96. It will be recalled that property was point two in Hegel's three-point outline. The property of the various branches of this family will be concentrated if the Major and Hilarie marry, and their offspring, if any, will have a larger inheritance, which in turn will decrease Flavio's share. This is not serious, however, for the widow he intends to marry is quite wealthy. The main mission of the tale is of course to break up the two age-to-youth pairings (Major-Hilarie; Flavio-widow) and recombine them age-to-age and youth-to-youth. Such a modified solution would also remain within the framework of the family, and that it is the correct one is indubitable in view of the Major's eventual "recollection" of a poem, the sense of which was: "Der späte Mond, der zur Nacht noch anständig leuchtet, verblaßt vor der aufgehenden Sonne; der Liebeswahn der Alters verschwindet in Gegenwart leidenschaftlicher Jugend"

† . . . while we take all kinds of trouble to make plans economically, natural affection plays such a trick on us.

‡ that affections of this kind are only apparent, that a kind of self-deception lies hidden behind them.

(p. 218).* To be noted particularly is what the correct realignment of couples does to questions of the family possessions: it will keep them within the family, but will spread them more evenly than the other solution. What Goethe, then, is saying in effect is that while considerations of family property are indeed important in arranging marriages—he spends much time in chapter 4 on their economic problems—they ought not to be controlling.

The primacy of family considerations is underlined by the magnificent scene before the painting of the family tree, in which the Major proposes to and is accepted by Hilarie (p. 180). It is significant that in one of the outlines that has been preserved Goethe sketched out a part of a family tree, apparently with the intention of including it in the story.[8] In this scene the following elements are to be distinguished: a) the consideration of how the transfer of Hilarie's affections from Flavio to the Major affect the financial plans of the family; b) how the family tree reflects the changing character of a family; c) how people of the same generation are referred to as if they "einander gerade ins Gesicht sehen" (look one another straight in the eye, p. 180), at which point Hilarie talks of "in die Höhe blicken" (looking upward); d) causing the major to propose and be accepted; e) what happens when the baroness enters and one learns that the Major has always been her favorite, which fact may have influenced the focusing of Hilarie's affections on him; f) how the three are united in an access of love and affection, at which they turn to thoughts of Flavio. The marvelous concentration of this scene, then, indicates that the family, in both the general and the specific sense, is the pivot on which the action of the tale turns.

It remains to note how the various errors arose and how they were corrected. In the Major's case his own male ego, his susceptibility to the flattering affection of an attractive girl, played a large role in bringing on the *Selbstbetrug* (self-deception) of which he ironically accused her (p. 166). When he was visited by an old actor friend, he was envious of the latter's youthful appearance, despite the fact that he was older than the Major. Then follows an amusing scene in which the Major persuades the actor to give him some of his magic cosmetics, while still avoiding reference to the real reason that he

---

* The late moon, which still shines quite decently at night, pales before the rising sun; the love-illusions of age disappear in the presence of passionate youth.

wanted them, namely, that he had fallen in love with a girl young enough to be his daughter. The actor not only gave him the cosmetics but also lent him the services of a special servant skilled in their use.[9] In other words, the Major got involved in questions of *Sein* and *Schein* (being and seeming), as his theatrical friend explained to him, and at the latter's advice and with the help of his "cosmetic servant," the fifty-year-old man tried to seem what he was not—a youth. The end of this aberration, the return to reality, is important, and is marked in two ways. First the cosmetic servant had to leave, from which time on the Major began to return to his former self; secondly, he was reminded that he was aging physically. In the various outlines mentioned above, Goethe included that as "Körperl. Uebel" (bodily ill[s]) in one, and in another as "Anmeldung der Gicht" (onset of rheumatism).[10] That the poet later changed this to the loss of a front tooth is a particularly adroit reminder that an element from the world of essentials (*Sein*) at the same time plays a most important role in the world of appearances (*Schein*)! In a final touch of irony the Major then received a letter from his theatrical friend informing him that the best way of preserving youthful appearances was to keep aloof from the fair sex!

In addition to the Major, Hilarie and Flavio also make emotional errors. The baroness reminded her brother, as they discussed Hilarie's affections, that youth often finds maturity attractive: "Es ist so unnatürlich nicht. . . . Aus meiner Jugend erinnere ich mich selbst einer Leidenschaft für einen älteren Mann als du bist" (p. 169).† In Flavio's case the intense competition of a large number of suitors for the hand of the beautiful widow had the effect of making her seem overwhelmingly attractive and at the same time aroused his masculine desire to win the competition for her hand (p. 182).

The two more mature ladies, however—the baroness and the beautiful widow—are depicted as knowledgeable and versed in the ways of the human heart. It was the baroness who first recognized the new magnet for her daughter's feelings, and who called it to the Major's attention. And it was this same sister who, long before anyone else, became uncomfortable at the age discrepancies between

---

† It isn't so unnatural. . . . From my youth I remember a passion for a man older than you are.

the two couples (p. 193) and turned to Makarie for advice, an act which was to have beneficial results. The beautiful widow herself was never deceived about a union between herself and Flavio; she never encouraged him, and from her first meeting with his father the Major she favored the latter. This may have been due in part at least to the fact that her first marriage had been to a much older man. At any rate it is significant that both of these wise ladies are shown habitually surrounded by unusually bright lights (pp. 186 and 200). And it is in darkness that the erring young Flavio came to them—he proposed to the widow in a dimly-lit ante-room, not in the bright drawing-rooms (p. 186)—and after being refused by her he burst out of the dark into the baroness's brightly lit rooms with a plea to be allowed to return to the dark (p. 203). This supposedly superior wisdom of women about other women is amusingly reflected in other language. Men are depicted as buyers who are not too well informed ("in the dark") about the "wares," whereas the women, like the merchants, are quite well aware of the value of the merchandise (p. 193). In other words, the superior knowledge of the baroness—and of Makarie—leads to an improvement of the situation, while the beautiful widow in her knowledge acts to prevent the situation from getting worse.

In addition, the amusing and appropriate motif of the widow's embroidery rests for its effectiveness on her superior knowledge of emotions. In those days it was customary for men to carry fabric letter cases in their pockets to hold important papers, and ladies of the time often embroidered such things for men of their family or friends. As a matter of fact, Goethe himself was the recipient of one from Johanna Fromann, wife of the Jena publisher in whose house he had been a frequent guest. We have his thank-you letter of 26 December 1807, in which he promises "meine liebsten Papierschätze . . . auf eine wunderliche Weise zu verwahren und zu produciren." ‡ [11] Then he went on that he hoped "was Sie an mir durch Nadelstiche gethan haben, durch Lettern und Silben zu erwiedern." * When the letter case is first mentioned (p. 184) the beautiful widow, up to now the object of son Flavio's affections, had been working on it for some time without having made up her mind

‡ to keep my dearest paper treasures . . . in a wonderful way and produce them.
* to reply with letters and syllables to what you have done for me with stitches.

definitely to whom to give it. Goethe had characterized her thus: "Sie war eins von den weiblichen Wesen, denen kein Mann entgeht" (p. 184).† An older friend of hers in the company smilingly claimed that the letter case was "ein penelopeisch zauderhaftes Werk," a piece of work delayed as Penelope delayed weaving her father-in-law's shroud. In the symbolic language our author loved, this means that the beautiful widow is looking for an appropriate man, but hasn't yet made up her mind who it will be, although it obviously won't be Flavio. The Major had been given the unfinished *Brieftasche* to admire at an evening party. The next morning when he comes to pay a farewell visit, he finds that in the few hours since the night before she had somehow found time to complete it! When she then gives it to him the symbolic meaning is obvious—the beautiful widow has found her man! She herself gives the key to the meaning of the embroidery:

Als junge Mädchen werden wir gewöhnt, mit den Fingern zu tifteln und mit den Gedanken umherzuschweifen; beides bleibt uns, idem wir nach und nach die schwersten und zierlichsten Arbeiten verfertigen lernen, und ich leugne nicht, daß ich an jede Arbeit dieser Art immer Gedanken angeknüpft habe. . . . Und so ward mir das Angefangene wert und das Vollendete, ich darf wohl sagen, kostbar. (p. 189) ‡

But the Major, as has been said, was a little slow. Even more interesting is the excuse she thought up for giving it to him. He has written a poem on hunting, which she claimed she wanted to read. So her letter case was to be used, she said, to enclose the poem as he sent it back to her, to guarantee that he really would send it. Symbolically this means, of course, that the hunter has not only been hunted, but netted! On his return home he sat down to dash off a verse of thanks to accompany his "Jagdgedicht" in the letter case. He chose to translate a verse from Ovid (Henkel claims that, characteristically, he did a clumsy job of translating):[12]

Das Schlimmste jedoch fiel ihm zuletzt ein: jene Ovidischen Verse werden von Arachnen gesagt, einer ebenso geschickten als hübschen und zierlichen Weberin. Wurde nun aber diese durch die neidische Minerva in eine Spinne

---

† She was one of those feminine beings that no man can escape.

‡ As young girls we become accustomed to work with our fingers and to wander with our thoughts; both (habits) remain with us as we gradually learn to finish the most difficult and graceful things, and I do not deny that I have always tied thoughts to every piece of work of this kind. . . . And so what I began was important to me and what I completed, I may say, precious.

verwandelt, so war es gefährlich, eine schöne Frau, mit einer Spinne, wenn auch nur von ferne, verglichen, im Mittelpunkte einer ausgebreiteten Netzes schweben zu sehen. (p. 198)*

But despite the fact that the Major recalled that it was Arachne, afterwards a spider, who spread her net, he never realized, being a little obtuse, that it was he himself who in this case was caught in a web! It is evident that Goethe was enjoying himself immensely when he wrote about the Major, the beautiful widow, and the letter case.

As has been done with all the other tales, the relationship to the ruler on the one hand and to the common people on the other must be examined. As far as the men, the Major and Flavio, are concerned, the relationship is presumed to have been good; both were military officers, which implied a degree of personal loyalty to the sovereign. Also the *Hofmarschall*, older brother to the Major and the baroness, was on terms of high favor with the widowed princess (p. 195). In view of her great social success, the widow must be assumed to have fitted well into the political world, which in those aristocratic days was closely allied to the social world.

The satisfactory relationship with the common people, however, one finds primarily with Flavio and Hilarie. After his recovery they both engaged in helping the populace, who had been afflicted with floods and freezing weather (pp. 210f). Thus successful integration upwards and downward in the milieu augurs well for the eventual happiness and success of the two marriages.

Parallels and contrasts with the other narrative inserts are many. In that the tale deals with the rectifications of emotional errors, it is reminiscent of the "Das nußbraune Mädchen" complex; in that the 1821 version contained only a beginning, to which the 1829 version contributed important additions, it is also similar to the same tale. Insofar as it depicts that attraction of a young woman for an older man it resembles the Hersilie-Wilhelm relationship of the main plot, or the between-the-generations cross of "Die pilgernde Törin." Trunz comments further: "Die Parallelen zu der 'Neuen Melusine'

---

* However the worst occurred to him at the end: those Ovid verses are said by Arachne, a weaver just as skillful as beautiful and graceful. If now she had been turned into a spider by the jealous Minerva, so it was dangerous to see a beautiful woman even distantly compared to a spider, hovering in the middle of a spread-out net.

und 'Nicht zu weit' (sowie zu den *Wahlverwandtschaften*) sind so zahlreich und deutlich, daß sie geradezu zur Frage an den Leser werden: warum gelingt hier die Harmonie und dort nicht?" (p. 664).† The reason is that here (in "Der Mann von funfzig Jahren") the proper background attitudes that affect the family as *Urform* and *Metamorphose* are either present or are attained, while in the case of "Die neue Melusine" and "Nicht zu weit" they are not.

The emotional errors of three of the lovers have been dealt with at some length. It is instructive to note the respective cures. In the case of Flavio the cure followed an emotional crisis that had the effect at the same time of a physical illness. That was relieved by bleeding, by nursing, and by the skillful therapeutic use of poetry by himself and by an attractive girl nurse, his future fiancée. Goethe described the beneficial effects thus: "Hier nun konnte die edle Dichtkunst abermals ihre heilenden Kräfte erweisen. Innig verschmolzen mit Musik, heilt sie alle Seelenleiden aus dem Grunde, indem sie solche gewaltsam anregt, hervorruft und in auflösenden Schmerzen verflüchtigt" (p. 206).‡

Finally close propinquity in service to the common people had an important part. A winter flood had isolated houses and villages, and Hilarie and Flavio had worked hard shoulder-to-shoulder to alleviate the suffering. Then a hard freeze had turned the landscape into a huge skating rink, where supplies and assistance could now move more easily. One moonlight night a symbolic scene took place. Hilarie and Flavio were having a fine time skating in circles, meeting and then parting, when an unidentified figure approached from the darkness. Hilarie was startled and fell, and when the Major went for a sled, for it was he, the young people (Hilarie wasn't hurt) sneaked away together. Here is another of what might be called the triangle pictures which Goethe sometimes used to sum up a tale. The final scene of "Nicht zu weit" shows a tragic human triangle of hate; the

---

† The parallels to "The New Melusine" and to "Not Too Far" (as well as to *The Elective Affinities*) are so numerous and clear that they actually comprise a question to the reader: why does harmony succeed here and not there?

‡ Here now once again the noble art of poetry could prove its healing powers. Intimately fused with music it heals all illnesses of the soul thoroughly by first powerfully producing and strengthening them, then dissipating them in dissolving pain.

Lenardo-Susanne-assistant triangle, beside the bed of her dying father in "Lenardos Tagebuch II," shows love.

Hilarie's cure on the other hand was not completed within the tale proper. It began as she looked on the sleeping Flavio, admired him, and suffered an outburst of jealousy for the widow. Later she was assisted in transferring her emotions from the father to the son by a) seeing the miniature of the father that resembled the son, and b) being struck by the resemblance of son for father as the son emerged from his sick room in his father's clothes. Devotion to the welfare of the common people also had a role, but the most important influence on her was doubtless art. She had considerable artistic gifts; from the first one hears that she is skillful on the piano, then she took up poetry in a kind of a metrical game encouraged by the physician to assist in Flavio's cure, but which also had its effect on her. The factor that was really decisive in her case came later when, in one of the postscripts (pp. 237–38), the reader learns that lessons and practice in drawing and sketching (at Lago Maggiore) had exercised a healing effect on her.

In conclusion, then, it can be said that the story shows that not any or every couple whose union had family sanction can attain happiness. The role of the family must be of the proper kind and concern the proper things. Property arrangements in a prospective marriage are important, but must not be allowed to become dominant. Questions of attraction and affection are primary, and to them the other considerations must be subordinated.

IX
WILHELM'S PREHISTORY

IN THE COMPLEX OF INSERTIONS that has been dealt with here as "Das nußbraune Mädchen," Lenardo's love for Nachodine, his development as a person, and more particularly hers, were seen to be the real subject matter. In the case of Wilhelm (ignoring the *Lehrjahre* and concentrating solely on the *Wanderjahre*), a somewhat similar but simpler situation is to be noted. Here there are only two parts: the story from his childhood and youth, which will be designated "Die Fischerknaben" ("The Fisherman's Boys," Book II, chapter 11, pp. 268–83), and his medical training (Book III, chapter 3, pp. 322–34). There is of course a major difference. Lenardo's contains the story of his love; Wilhelm's deals primarily with his decision for and his training in the profession of medicine. Furthermore the three parts of Lenardo's are set off from the main plot, each with its own title; neither of Wilhelm's are. In Lenardo's narrative, the largest of the metamorphoses of the family, the industrious mountain weaver *Volk*, play an important role. Likewise in the first part of Wilhelm's insertion the populace of the country, the city, and even larger circles play a similar role.

Waidson terms the "Die Fischerknaben" the focal point of the novel,[1] which in a very real sense it is, and this constitutes the internal linkage. It will be recalled that Goethe has been depicting the effect of passion on an individual with the inflicting of a wound, either physical or psychological—a wound which tended to isolate the injured subject.[2] To cure the affected one, and to restore him to society, a physician is highly desirable. It will be recalled further that Wilhelm had had a vision while under Makarie's influence, of his own future mission: "Ich soll erforschen, was edle Seelen auseinanderhält, soll Hindernisse wegräumen, von welcher Art sie auch seien" (p. 119).* And when Wilhelm will have attained the

---

* I am to find out what keeps noble souls apart, I am to remove the hindrances of whatever kind they may be.

WILHELM'S PREHISTORY 69

status of physician, then he will have become, in the abbé's words, "[das] notwendigste Glied unserer Kette" ([the] most necessary link of our chain, p. 243). In this sense, then, the impulses that originally channeled Wilhelm's interests towards this profession of medicine are of key importance.

There has already been occasion to point to the care Goethe used in "framing" various of the narrative elements. This is particularly important in the "Fischerknaben." As was the case with "St. Joseph II," the tale is told in one of Wilhelm's letters to Natalie, and the material addressed directly to her opens and closes the insertion, forming frame 1, so to speak (268.1–23 and 282.32 to 283.5). A portion of the letter contains a reference to the very important *Ruderpflock* (thole pin, 268.10–23 and 280.17 to 282.31), which thus forms an inner frame, frame 2. Then immediately "inside" the *Ruderpflock* references there are three general observations at the beginning and one such at the end, making, so to speak, frame 3. The situation is complicated, however, by the fact that three of these general observations, some of which could be called aphorisms, come in the middle of the tale, an unusual place to find framing elements.

There are further linkages.[3] In the second part of frame 2 Wilhelm referred to one of his earlier conversations with Montan at the *Kohlenmeiler* (charcoal kiln) and quoted a significant portion of it (281.1 to 282.32). This is interesting, because another similar serious conversation with Montan—they all concerned choice of profession—is quoted at the end of Book II, chapter 9 (262.17 to 264.29), in other words shortly before the beginning of "Die Fischerknaben," separated from it by chapter 10. This becomes even more interesting in view of the fact that serious conversations about the choice of profession are used to frame the report on Wilhelm's medical training (322.24–35 and 331.1 to 334.14) and to join it to "Die Fischerknaben," frame A (pp. 262, 281, 322, 331). If one then considers as frame 1 the letter to Natalie (pp. 268, 283), as frame 2 the *Ruderpflock* (pp. 268, 280) and as frame 3 the aphorisms (pp. 268–9, 273–4, 279–80), and further puts the nonrelated material in square brackets, one gets the following linear sequence:

A [chap. 10] (1 (2 (3 (*Fischer*) 3 (*-knaben*) 3) 2) (A) 1) [chap. 1,2] A) medical ed.

However, Goethe does not make things too simple: the last portion of frame A develops naturally out of the enclosed narrative so that one can see content and frame intermingled while the author makes a few significant points as the tale ends. Thus it is obvious that Goethe has not only carefully set off each part with his framing technique, but has also linked the two insertions together in the same way. And yet he has not provided either of them, nor the whole, with a title! There will be occasion later to consider the reasons for this.

The external linkage is quite simple; it makes up the subject matter of a long and discursive letter to Natalie, and so one sees a significant relationship to "St. Joseph II." Thus it flows out of the main plot easily, and it passes just as easily back into it, for at the end of the second part both Lenardo and Friedrich interrupt (p. 333), and the tale passes naturally from narrative to a general conversation on the problems involved and then back into the main plot. Two other facts are of interest here: the continuation—medical studies—is not a letter, is not addressed to Natalie, but it is a story told orally to the other members of the group. Even more interesting is the fact that in *form* the first part, "Die Fischerknaben," is told in the first person throughout, while the second starts out as such, shifts to the third person (p. 324), then back to the first person for the ending (p. 332). These external differences give the reader the impression that the poet was trying to disguise the fact, rather than emphasize it, that the two elements essentially belong together, in which respect it resembles the dissimilarity in title and tone between "Das nußbraune Mädchen" and "Lenardos Tagebuch."

The *Ruderpflock* frame[4] constitutes an explanation for the whole story, really a parable, of the fisherman's boys: the thole pin reminds Wilhelm of his *Besteck* (case of surgical instruments) and what that meant in his life. In the *Lehrjahre* Wilhelm and his group of actors had been ambushed by bandits, and Wilhelm was left unconscious on the ground with a serious head wound. When he came to he found his head on the lap of a beautiful girl—a noble family had stopped to render aid—and as Wilhelm fell in love with the girl (it was Natalie), her family *Wundarzt* (barber-surgeon) tended to him with this same *Besteck*. In later years he had acquired the instrument case, which served him as a double reminder, first of his love, and secondly of the profession he had determined to follow—medicine.

WILHELM'S PREHISTORY

Frame 3, the aphorism-like generalities, is of crucial importance. The second generality is to the effect that young men are fortunate if they can follow in the professional footsteps of their fathers. This anticipates the second half of the tale, where the work of Wilhelm's father to improve the health of the city has obviously helped inspire Wilhelm's medical ambitions. The three central aphorisms (273.25 to 274.9) are reflections on the meaning of the first half of the story; the one at the end (279.28 to 280.7) comments on the significance of the entire tale. It should not be overlooked that on the next page begins "Betrachtungen im Sinne der Wanderer," ("Reflections according to the Travelers"), a collection consisting of 26 pages, 177 individual aphorisms, *practically any one of which* could be a reflection on the meaning of a narrative, except that with this collection the narratives are not given. It is up to the reader—at least that is the wordless suggestion—to invent a tale appropriate for each! This opens up various possibilities, to which it will be necessary to return.

The "Fischerknaben" tale is the account of city-born Wilhelm's first excursion into the country, how he meets the fisherman's son Adolf, goes swimming, and establishes his first friendship. That same afternoon a blond country girl captures his attention. The two adolescents are strongly drawn to each other and wander hand-in-hand through a flower garden. Brown has shown how the flowers they admired, or anticipated,[5] bloom in succession from spring through autumn, which is also, of course, a symbolic reference to the ages of man, from youth to old age.

In the second half of the tale Wilhelm is then crushed by the news of the accidental drowning of his new friend Adolf and his brothers; friendship, love, and death have then confronted him, all for the first time and all on the same day. Following that he tells of his aunt, a lively, parsimonious woman, a born lobbyist in obtaining favors from city government, and of her influential contact there, a man of elastic scruples, it would seem, plus a taste for delicacies. If the account of the aunt and her friends paints a rather uncomplimentary picture of the middle-class society of the city (Goethe was basing this on his native Frankfurt, of course), the following description of his father's activities more than counterbalances it:

Mein Vater war jener Zeit einer der ersten, der seine Betrachtung, seine Sorge über die Familie, über die Stadt hinaus zu erstrecken durch einen allgemeinen, wohlwollenden Geist getrieben ward. Die großen Hindernisse, welche der Einimpfung der Blattern anfangs entgegenstanden, zu beseitigen, war er mit verständigen Ärzten und Polizeibeamten bemüht. Größere Sorgfalt in den Hospitälern, menschlichere Behandlung der Gefangenen und was sich hieran ferner schließen mag, machte das Geschäft, wo nicht seines Lebens, doch seines Lesens und Nachdenkens; wie er denn auch seine Überzeugung überall aussprach und dadurch manches Gute bewirkte. (p. 278)†

There has been little in this insertion to recall the family as *Urform* (with the exception of the family visit to the country), but with Wilhelm's father all of a sudden the larger metamorphoses thereof, the city and the larger populace beyond, become the center of attention, which is all the more significant when one considers that Wilhelm's profession of medicine is considered as a service to that larger society (*Volk*).

Finally his father's view of society is vital: "Er sah die bürgerliche Gesellschaft, welcher Staatsform sie auch untergeordnet wäre, als einen Naturzustand an, der sein Gutes und sein Böses habe, seine gewöhliche Lebensläufe, abwechselnd reiche und kümmerliche Jahre, nicht weniger zufällig und unregelmäßig Hagelschlag, Wasserfluten und Brandschäden." (p. 278).‡ From pantheist Goethe this means then that human society (the largest metamorphosis of the *Urform* family) was just as justifiably an object of scientific study and treatment as were rocks (geology) or plants (botany).

The last portion of this account of Wilhelm's prehistory concerns a large part of his medical training. In Goethe's day there was a distinction between the lowly *Wundarzt* or *Chirurg* (barber-surgeon) who was without university education, and who did the obvious external things (*Chirurg* is from the Greek, meaning "hand work")

† My father was one of the first at that time who was driven by a general and beneficial spirit to extend his attention and his concern beyond the family, beyond the city. He, with understanding physicians and police officials, made an effort to eliminate the great hindrances which stood at the beginning in the way of smallpox vaccination. Greater care in the hospitals, more humane treatment of prisoners, and other things of this kind, these things made up, if not the business of his life, at least of his reading and reflection. He also expressed his convictions everywhere and thereby accomplished a lot of good.

‡ He considered middle-class society, whatever the form of state it was subjected to, as a natural condition which had its good side and its bad, its regular vicissitudes of life, good years and poverty-stricken ones in rotation, no less accidentally and irregularly [than] hailstorms, floods and conflagrations.

like bandaging, setting broken bones, bleeding patients, etc., and the university-educated *Arzt* or *Leibarzt* (physician), who dealt with diseases and their history, prescribed drugs, diets, baths, etc. It is noteworthy that Goethe restricted his hero to the lower, in conformity with his ideal of craftsmanship.

However, it is only a part of Wilhelm's training that is described here, the manufacture and use in instruction of anatomical models, rather than the dissection of cadavers. But Wilhelm had done dissection, and his recommendation was that the models be used by beginners, and by older, practising physicians who needed to refresh their knowledge. He specifically leaves open resort to dissection "in der mittleren Zeit" (in the time in between, p. 333). Wilhelm had learned at Makarie's (p. 119) that he was to function as *Seelenarzt* (physician of the soul) in helping found families. Here he becomes a *Wundarzt* and moreover one who specializes as an artist and as a teacher. As a craftsman-artist he builds the models, and then uses them in instruction. These are the skills, then, that he is to take across the ocean and put to use in service of the new society in the new world.

X
"DIE NEUE MELUSINE"

IN BOOK 10 OF *Dichtung und Wahrheit* (*Poetry and Truth*, Goethe's autobiography), in a part written in 1811, he speaks of entertaining the family of Friederike Brion in Sesenheim (near Strassburg) in 1771 with a version of this tale. It was not written down, however, until much later: he mentioned it in a letter to Schiller in 1791,[1] then wrote it in 1807, to publish it in 1816. He is quite specific about the fact that the published version differed from the one Friederike heard:

> Leider werde ich es [das Märchen] jetzo in seiner ersten unschuldigen Freiheit nicht überliefern. Es ist lange nachher aufgeschrieben worden und deutet in seiner jetzigen Ausbildung an eine reifere Zeit als die ist, mit der wir uns dort beschäftigten. So viel reiche hin, um den einseitigen Hörer vorzubereiten. Sollte ich also gegenwärtig jenes Märchen erzählen, so würde ich folgendergestalt anfangen. (9.745)*

The title and the main outline he took from the chapbook story "Die schöne Melusine,"[2] which in turn goes back to a French original of 1387. This details a part of the story of the French noble house of Lusignan: the name Melusine is supposedly derived from "mère de Lusignan." However, there were other influences. Fink has marshalled the source materials and shown convincingly when each probably entered into this expanding body of material that Goethe carried in his mind for some forty-five years before it saw print.[3] From the loving attention to detail it is also evident that this fairytale was a favorite of the author's.

It is narrated by the silent barber and has no less than two intro-

---

* Unfortunately I will not transmit it [the tale] now in its first innocent freedom. It was written down long afterward and in its present development indicates a much more mature time than that with which we were dealing there [in his autobiography]. May so much suffice to prepare the one-sided reader. If I were to tell that fairy-tale at present, then I would begin in the following fashion.

ductions: the first introduces the narrator (pp. 352-3), and with the second the narrator introduces his tale (354.1-22). The most cursory examination of the story shows that it is a negative example, and it is just this that the narrator warns the reader about in his introduction:

Ich war in meiner Jugend kein guter Wirt und fand mich oft in mancherlei Verlegenheit. Einst nahm ich mir eine Reise vor, die mir guten Gewinn verschaffen sollte; aber ich machte meinen Zuschnitt ein wenig zu gross, und nachdem ich sie mit Extrapost angefangen und sodann auf der ordinären eine Zeitlang fortgesetzt hatte, fand ich mich zuletzt genötigt, dem Ende derselben zu Fuße entgegenzugehen. (p. 354)†

As the narration begins one notices the framing technique in use again. The hero tells how, when forced to economize, he made it a practice to devote himself especially to the cook in every house or inn into which he came, having found that such attentiveness would guarantee him more and better food for his money. At the end of this adventure, having apparently learned and profited nothing, he finds himself back in a kitchen flattering a cook, as he noted wryly, "durch einen ziemlichen Umweg" (via a considerable detour, p. 376).

On first impression the story seems to be little more than a charming piece of make-believe. Our penniless hero makes himself useful to a beautiful and wealthy girl traveling alone, who engages him to carry and care for a special box she takes everywhere. Propinquity quickly develops into love. He doesn't find it out until later, but she is really a princess of the dwarfs, sent out into the world of humans to find a lover so that the dwarf race, which has been getting too small, can get a needed infusion of human blood! The box turns out to be a tiny, completely furnished dwarf-sized parlor, to which she retreats secretly at times.

The external linkage is Lenardo's introduction, which identifies the narrator as the barber, "ein derber Wundarzt" (a hearty barber-surgeon) and also a member of the group. Lenardo describes the man as skillful in amusing his listeners with his tales—and the element of legend in them is suggestive—but more important, Lenardo holds

† In my youth I was not a good manager, and often found myself in many kinds of embarrassment. Once I set out on a trip that was supposed to bring me a good profit; but I set my style a little too high, and after I had begun it with a special carriage, and then had continued it for a time with the regular one, I finally found myself forced to end it on foot.

out as exemplary the self-control by which the barber refrains from all conversation while working so as to be able to concentrate more skillfully on the telling of stories. This is in significant contrast to the hero's lack of self-control in the story itself. And the reader is specifically notified that although the tale is in the form of a legend, which provides for the inclusion of art and reflection, it is constructed on the experiences of the narrator, and is thus a kind of *Dichtung und Wahrheit* (p. 353). The narrative insertion, however, ends abruptly; there is no further attempt to link it to the main plot.

In *form* the cyclical element here is of great importance, as it was in "Wer ist der Verräter?" The dwarf princess incognito tells him that she has tested many candidates for her love, and only he is suited, although it is hardly clear why. She places several conditions on their continued association, all of which he manages to ignore. Although he realizes that the girl does not care for any affectionate embrace, he cannot control himself and throws his arms around her (p. 356); he then becomes careless with money (p. 357); although she warns him, he gets involved with wine and women (pp. 358–59); although he has promised not to betray her secret, not to indulge in anger or wine, he then proceeded to do all these (p. 365). Then without marriage they begin to live together. At the end, although he had gotten her pregnant, become a dwarf so as to live with her and her people, and even married her, he finally broke all those ties, returned to his human size and deserted her, her people, and her child to come, and even squandered the gifts which she, despite everything, had sent after him.

The hero is actively hostile at first to the idea of marriage, and most interestingly he links this idea to an aversion to music: "Wie schrecklich ward mir auf einmal zu mute, als ich von Heirat reden hörte: denn ich fürchtete mich bisher davor fast mehr als vor der Musik selbst, die mir doch sonst das Verhaßtete auf Erden schien" (p. 373).‡ He went on to specify that what repelled him about music was that it required mutual agreement, unity, and harmony. This is all the more interesting for the fact that at one point our hero found himself *liking* music. After he had gotten drunk, gotten angry, and had betrayed her secret, he repented, "Ich erkannte den grossen

‡ How terribly I felt suddenly when I heard talk of marrying, because I was almost more afraid of that than of music itself, which otherwise seemed to me the most hateful thing in the world.

Fehler, den ich begangen hatte, und war recht innerlich zerknirscht. Zum erstenmal sprach die Musik mich an" (p. 365),* and he enjoyed her song of farewell. When, then, he was his selfish, hedonistic, individualistic, and irresponsible self, music was anathema to him. When, however, he humbled himself and regretted his errors, music became pleasant. But this was only the last of several repentances of his, none of which had lasted very long. It is the repeated errors that prove him unsuited for founding a family; it is the repeated but short-lived repentances and reformations, it is the hostility to marriage and to music that constitute the internal linkage of the tale.

In each story the relationship of the couple to the social and political superiors and inferiors has been revealing. It should be noted that the dwarf princess's description of the creation and mission of the dwarf world was entirely favorable (pp. 367–69). They are creatures of God and have a place of honor and utility in his creation; there is nothing of the demonic, nothing pejorative or derogatory about them. On becoming a dwarf, then, the hero was not demeaning himself. The noteworthy fact is that the hero cannot stay on good terms with either the dwarf rulers or with the people, which, in view of what we have been observing Goethe to show about the family, is what one would expect in view of the faulty nature of his character. When he resumed human form, he found himself "freilich um so vieles grösser, allein, wie mir vorkam, auch um vieles dümmer und unbehülflicher" (p. 375).†

There is an even more interesting problem here. To explain her presence among mankind, the princess tells of the decision of the wise old men to counteract the unhealthy tendency among them to become too small, and "daß von Zeit zu Zeit eine Prinzessin aus dem königlichen Hause heraus ins Land gesendet werde, um sich mit einem ehrsamen Ritter zu vermählen, damit das Zwergengeschlecht wieder angefrischt und vom gänzlichen Zerfall gerettet sei" (p. 368).‡ But exactly how is the marriage of the princess alone going to exert a beneficial influence on the entire race of dwarfs? The

---

* I recognized the great mistake that I had committed, and was inwardly quite contrite. For the first time music appealed to me.

† to be sure so much the larger, but, as it seemed to me, also much dumber and clumsier.

‡ that from time to time a princess from the royal house is sent out into the country in order to marry an honorable knight so that the race of dwarfs can be again renewed and saved from complete ruin.

only possible conclusion, since we are in the legendary world, is that there was some kind of a magical relationship between the marriage of the ruler and the well-being of the subjects. This is the equivalent in the fairy-tale world to the beneficial influence that ruler's happy marriage exerts on the relationship to his people, which was to be seen in "St. Joseph II," "Wer ist der Verräter?" and in a limited degree "Der Mann von funfzig Jahren."

Thus what seemed at the beginning to be nothing more than an attractive exercise in fairy-tale invention turns out to be at the same time a fairly thorough documentation of the fact that the hero lacks the qualities needed to establish a marriage and moreover possesses vices calculated to destroy one. He drinks, he gambles, he chases strange women, he fights, and he lacks self-control, and thus the tale is in sharp, polar, contrast to those narrative insertions that have ended with the hero's successful marriage or the prospect of one: "Sankt Joseph der Zweite," Lucidor in "Wer ist der Verräter?" Lenardo in "Das nußbraune Mädchen," and the Major and Flavio in "Der Mann von funfzig Jahren." They are able to practice renunciation, which our hero was not. Insofar as the tale depicts an unsuccessful marriage it is similar to "Nicht zu weit," although here the husband, not the wife, is at fault.

In view of what has been noted in the other tales, it is quite possible that the negative comments on the hero's qualities as a family man are part of Goethe's later additions to the tale, which the little group around Friederike in the arbor at Sesenheim in 1771 did not hear.

XI
"DIE GEFÄHRLICHE WETTE"

THIS INSERTION has been a stumbling block for most critics and interpreters because it does not fit easily into either the series of other novellas or into the main plot of the novel. The most obvious difference from the other novellas is that it does not contain a love affair. Some commentators have merely ignored it. Although Riemann liked the tale,[1] he thought it was "badly fitted" into the novel. One, the socialist Gregorovius,[2] saw the reason for the tale's existence to prove that the hero Christoph was a true proletarian (because of the fact that he carried burdens). Klingenberg[3] sees the tale's purpose as related to "Die pädagogische Provinz": the hero lacks the second of the three reverences, that due one's fellow man. Wolff[4] thought the hero's sin was *Übermut* (arrogant, wild spirits), the effects of which lead to tragedy, and Brown[5] takes the similar but more general view that Christoph's error is asocial behaviour. Furthermore Trunz points out that one cannot dismiss the tale as unimportant. Goethe originally wrote it in 1807, did not include it in the 1821 version, then made some rather far-reaching changes in the final, 1829 version, which proves beyond doubt that the story's inclusion in the novel was anything but an accident. There was conscious artistic purpose behind it.

The material is introduced in a superficial way, to say the least. The "editor" says that he is introducing "einen Schwank, den wir ohne weitere Vorbereitung hier einschalten, weil unsere Angelegenheiten immer ernsthafter werden und wir für dergleichen Unregelmässigkeiten fernerhin keine Stelle finden möchten" (p. 378).* This stimulated Klingenberg's ingenuity, as follows: Goethe foresaw that

---

* a farce which we want to insert here without further preparation, because our affairs are becoming more and more serious and we might not find further along a place for such irregularities.

there would be objection to this tale on the ground that it did not fit, so he made fun of that stupid objection by giving in advance an even stupider reason for including it![6] There is an interesting possibility that Goethe intended the reader to see the use of the frame here. Christoph begins his story with an aphorism-like comment: "Es ist bekannt, daß die Menschen, sobald es ihnen einigermaßen wohl und nach ihrem Sinne geht, alsbald nicht wissen, was sie vor Übermut anfangen sollen" (p. 383).† Then at the end he says, "Da nun jede Fabel eigentlich etwas lehren soll, so ist euch allen, wohin die gegenwärtige gemeint sein, wohl überklar und deutlich" (p. 383).‡ In other words, instead of ending with an aphorism to neatly close the frame, he suggests the reader supply one to fit the tale! And the same aphorism at the beginning does double duty, as it were, by putting all on notice that this is to be another negative example.

Christoph is with a group of students at an inn when he notices the arrival of a wealthy aristocrat who happens to have a large nose. With sudden inspiration: "What do you bet," he challenges the others, "that I can pull that man's nose this way and that without making him angry?" After collecting the wagered money, he ingratiates himself as a barber's apprentice with the nobleman and shaves him, during the process of which, of course, he makes an opportunity to turn the gentleman's head by his nose. The students laugh uproariously, but the noble gentleman, when he finally finds out how he has been ridiculed, flies into a rage that endangers them all. The external linkage is that this is one of the documents from the collection, which is also clearly from the biography of "saint" Christopher ("meine Riesenkraft" [my giant strength], 382.31). To this extent it is parallel to "Das nußbraune Mädchen," "Die Fischerknaben," "Der Man von funfzig Jahren," and "Die neue Melusine." There is no love story here: the dominant passions are the opposite of love—ridicule and anger. And there is an interesting minor point that links this to the previous negative example "Die neue Melusine": both heroes are left-handed!

† It is well known that people, as soon as they are well off and things are going their way, forthwith don't know, from pure arrogant wild spirits, what to do next.

‡ Since every tale really is supposed to teach something, so it is probably more than clear and obvious to all of you in what direction the present one is intended.

DIE GEFÄHRLICHE WETTE

To the extent that a central theme of the tale is the hero's thoughtless self-indulgence at the expense of others, this account is parallel to "Die neue Melusine," as it is also in the fact that uncontrolled anger plays a destructive role. As Seidlin notes,[7] Goethe has unobtrusively established several links between the two tales: both are *Icherzählungen*; both heroes function as barbers, and both are giants—Christoph really, the Melusine hero at least in comparison with the dwarf world. There is no direct reference to the family, nor to the social superiors and inferiors, but it is interesting to note how the social classes are depicted. Christoph and most of his friends are of the middle class, while Raufbold and the strange gentleman are of the nobility. It is the nobles who cannot forget the "insult," and it is their exaggerated sense of honor that leads to the old gentleman's death and the duel between his son and Raufbold. The form is, if anything, dramatic: that of the practical joke that has tragic results.

The strongest contrast here is not only between love and anger, it is also between the irresponsible, hedonistic students of the tale who are selfish, self-centered, and almost without ties or responsibilities, and the serious and hard-working members of the emigrating group around Lenardo. As a matter of fact this is the internal linkage of the tale, and the moral mentioned at the end of the story (383.29–30) is doubtless the fact that through this experience Christoph has learned to quit using his huge strength (and quick wit) only for his own amusement and come to devote them instead to the service of others, as he has been seen to do in "Lenardos Tagebuch I," in aiding and supporting social organizations.

There are two other points of view from which this farce is interesting. There has been occasion to note Goethe's predilection, resulting from his scientific studies, to think in series. Among the novellas in this novel that he has provided with a title, all but one, "Die gefährliche Wette," contain a love story, and it should not be overlooked that at the beginning Goethe had his "editor" call it "eine Unregelmässigkeit" (an irregularity). There are also a number of other insertions of narrative nature in the novel that are untitled and that do not contain a love affair—with one exception. There is thus a symmetry between the two series, in each of which the exception suggests or points to the other series, thus:

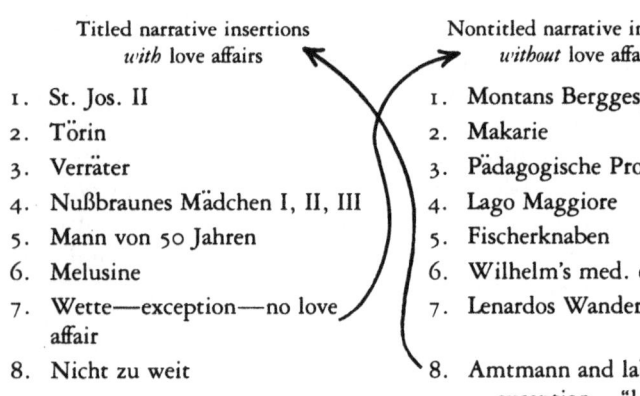

Titled narrative insertions *with* love affairs	Nontitled narrative insertions *without* love affairs
1. St. Jos. II	1. Montans Berggespräche
2. Törin	2. Makarie
3. Verräter	3. Pädagogische Provinz
4. Nußbraunes Mädchen I, II, III	4. Lago Maggiore
5. Mann von 50 Jahren	5. Fischerknaben
6. Melusine	6. Wilhelm's med. ed.
7. Wette—exception—no love affair	7. Lenardos Wanderrede
8. Nicht zu weit	8. Amtmann and labor force —exception—"love" affairs
	9. American utopia

The fact has been noted that the "Wette" insertion ends with an invitation to the reader to construct his own moral for the tale, a moral that could easily take the form of an aphorism. Previously, in the middle and at the end of "Die Fischerknaben," there was occasion to note how the general remarks similar to aphorisms commented on or summed up a part or all of the narration. If one considers the hint that the reader make his own aphorism in connection with the two large collections of aphorisms in the novel, the possibility must be considered: Did Goethe include the collections of proverbs in the novel as a way of silently inviting the reader to invent an appropriate narrative to go with each? If, as seems certain, Goethe meant to narrate his novel from many different perspectives, then this would seem to be the best available explanation for the fact that he included the collections. Thus "Die gefährliche Wette" is in a way a double transition: first from the titled, love-affair series of narrative insertions to the nontitled, non–love-affair series; and secondly from the narratives with expressed or implied aphorism-like morals to the aphorisms alone, whose explanatory narratives are to be supplied.

There was occasion to note above that a "family" might consist of a non–blood-related group, for instance the weaver or spinner folk in the mountain valleys, or the students and instructors in the pedagogical province. It was likewise noted that, in the series of subplots that contained love affairs, "Nicht zu weit" fills the function of a negative example. Comparably, in the series of non-blood-related families in the novel, "Die gefährliche Wette" functions also as a negative example. With "Melusine," that makes three negative examples that the poet has placed near the end of his novel; this is graphically illustrated in the outline on pages 144–45.

XII
"NICHT ZU WEIT"

ALTHOUGH IT IS the next to the last novella in the work, this one still offers some new problems, for Goethe, as has been noted, likes to innovate. Here he has the hero Odoard introduce himself in a way that turns out to be characteristic. When first asked to speak to the assemblage, he declined diplomatically until he had a chance to introduce himself and his ideas properly to its leaders (p. 384). In other words, Odoard acts like a person used to disciplined subordination and proper respect for authority. He declines to try to recruit someone else's subordinates without first "going through channels" in the way he would want others to approach his subordinates.

Next the "editor" explained how he had happened to get a copy of the manuscript of this story (p. 393), which could function very nicely as the first part of a frame around the tale, and in the *Wanderjahre* Goethe frequently used the frame technique with his narrative insertions. On examination it becomes clear, however, that, although the "editor" breaks in repeatedly during the action of the plot, there is nothing to close the frame, so to speak, at the end. Gidion sees this,[1] as well as the fact that there are no less than six obtrusions of the frame into the tale. This, by the way, aids Goethe in achieving a frequent change of perspective. The omniscient narrator starts, then Odoard takes over in the first person, then the tale is taken up again by the narrator, then the old nurse reports, and so on. In addition there are two flash-backs, so that frequent interruptions by the frame serve to divide the tale into compartments, as it were. Riemann, who does not see what Goethe is trying to do, says:[2] "Hier tritt völlige Wirrnis ein" [Here complete confusion sets in].

This entire insertion is also, of course, a negative model. It ends with the tragic triangle-picture of the scorned Albertina crowded into the carriage seat with her deceivers, "und in der Hölle selbst könnten widerwertige Gesinnte, Verratene mit Verrätern so eng nicht zusammengepackt sein" (p. 404).* There are two nonconnected narrative strands in this tale, the Odoard strand and the Albertina strand. It is plain that the author has taken some pains to shape the novella to make this scene the climactic one, despite the fact that it is only about one third of the way through the Albertina strand. Therefore any appearance of a framing element thereafter would necessarily have an anticlimactic effect, and hence he avoided it.

Both von Monroy and Henkel believe that they can detect a difference between the Odoard of the main plot and the Odoard of the novella.[3] It was noted earlier how Odoard had identified himself right at the first, before the tale began, as an authoritarian. During the action there are two further chances to see his absolutist side. One learns first that he been educated in a military academy (p. 396), where of course discipline and respect for authority are inculcated. Secondly since he was popular and experienced at court and in diplomacy, he was clearly a promising young man. Consequently the prime minister had married his daughter to him—a marriage for power and prestige rather than for love, and acquiesced in by Odoard as a good, if ambitious, subordinate. That this is in contrast to the ideal marriage of St. Joseph II at the beginning of the novel is obvious. Then, after the plot of the *Novelle* is over Odoard holds a long recruiting speech in which he appears as a reform-minded conservative, bent on imposing reform from above.[4] But he is still a believer in absolutism, as is to be seen most obviously from the song his departing "Einwanderer" [immigrants, as opposed to emigrants] sing, of which more later. In other words, he is in fact the same consistent character throughout.

The novella appears only in the final version of the novel, and was written in 1825 and 1826. More interesting are the models that might have inspired Goethe. Both Beutler and Deiters[5] see his brother-in-law Schlosser as Goethe's model, although the former's comparable experiences began some fifty-two years before Goethe came to write this account. There could have been other influences: Sagave notes that Eisenach was an enclave of Saxe-Weimar, and could have served as model, but the little duchy at that time had

* and in hell itself contrarily minded people, betrayed with the betrayers, couldn't be packed together so tightly.

other enclaves as well, any of which Goethe could have had in mind, and all of which he must have known intimately.[6] It is known that there was not only an actual model for the American settlement that Lenardo's group was to found, but also that the government of Württemberg had set up a land development project in Württemberg to offer attractive opportunities to possible emigrants and thus keep them at home.[7] Goethe certainly knew about these.

Critics have pointed out that there are really two plot lines in the tale, the Odoardo line and the Albertina one, and that the two never really coalesce.[8] And the same critics have objected to the fact that the story doesn't come to a climax or resolution. To be sure the reader does not find out either what happened to Odoard and his Aurora, or how Albertina solved her troubles. However, if it was Goethe's intention to show the mutual agony and heartbreak that can come from a broken marriage, then the Albertina plot and the Odoard plot should *not* intersect, and the place Goethe chose to stop shows that most effectively. More would be anticlimactic.

This semifinal narrative insertion is in contrast in meaning and in position to "Sankt Joseph der Zweite"; the ideal model came at the beginning, while this last tale is one of unrelieved tragedy and is a model of what is wrong, erroneous, and to be avoided in marriage and family life. Odoard had prepared a festive dinner for his wife Albertina's birthday; the children had memorized versified birthday greetings, but their mother did not appear. After a long wait the father turned the children over to their nurse and retreated to a local inn, where, to explain his presence, he invented a tale about some friends who might arrive later.

Meanwhile Albertina, who had been out in the country dancing with her best woman friend and her *Hausfreund* (house friend, euphemism for a tolerated lover) had had a carriage accident on the way home. From the reactions of the others to the emergency, Albertina had suddenly realized that her *Hausfreund* and her lady friend had been deceiving her and were lovers.

The external linkage to the main plot is the fact that, at the beginning, so as to identify himself and the legitimacy of his recruitment, Odoard tells his tale to the other leaders. At the *end* the story also trails off into the main plot, in Odoard's recruitment speech and song (pp. 408–13). In form a strange mixture of dramatic and epic styles is to be seen. The narration starts off in the third person, but shifts to the first person for a peak of emotion, as Odoard says of Albertina: "Ich fing an, sie zu hassen" (I began to hate her, p. 394). One other negative example, "Die gefährliche Wette," centers on the emotion of anger. When the author then shifts back to the third person, it is with a heavily ironic tone: "die Rechte des epischen Dichters uns anmassend" (assuming the rights of the epic poet, p. 395). The next bit of narrative in the first person is the speech of the children's old nurse. It is this speech that contains the title: "Ich sagt' es ihr mehr als einmal, sie solle es nicht zu weit treiben" (p. 396) [I told her more than once she shouldn't push it too far]. Then the narrative returns to the third person again as Odoard heard the surprising news that the out-of-town guests whom he had invented to explain his presence at the inn, or people the servants took for them, had actually arrived. This passage is quite short (p. 399), and the reason for putting it into the first person is to reflect his emotional tension. The author then relapses to the third person for the remainder of the tale.

It is now in order to examine a number of contrasts to what we have already seen, and this really constitutes the internal linkage to the central plot of the novel. Valid marriages are founded on love; in this indifference and hate dominate (p. 394). It has been noted that Goethe laid great stress on the education of "Sankt Joseph der Zweite," and of Lucidor in "Wer ist der Verräter?" Favorable things are said about Lenardo's educational tour, and of course about Felix in the pedagogical province, and about Wilhelm and his medical studies. Odoard, however, had been trained in a military school (p. 396). That the creator of the pedagogical province would have had a low opinion of such an institution hardly needs proof.

Then the reader learns that Odoard had contracted an arranged marriage with Albertina for reasons of family politics. It has been observed how, in "Der Mann von funfzig Jahren" and in "Wer ist der Verräter?," family reasons have a valid part to play in arranging marriages, so long as they are consistent with the feelings of the couple concerned. It should not be overlooked that Odoard's interest in Princess Sophronie continued after his marriage to Albertina (p. 397); there was thus no love on either side between Odoard and Albertina.

When, then, the Aurora poem was discovered and the enemies of Odoard and his family caused trouble, Odoard was banished from court, in effect, by being made regent of a distant enclave, completely surrounded by lands of other sovereignties. And the entire influence of his father-in-law was required to achieve even this solution. Throughout we have noted that a good marriage and family relationship as Goethe described it made desirable a successful integration into larger social spheres, harmony with both social superiors and inferiors. In Odoard's case the relationship to the superiors is on a very shaky basis. Nothing is heard of the relationship to the common people. What is indicated, as for instance in the song, is that Odoard gave orders on almost all matters, even on the marriage of the young people. The personal reaction of the people concerned is not mentioned.

But Odoard had to cope with other sources of resistance to his plans: his wife was disinterested and bored in the provincial town, and the conservative and old-fashioned politics of neighboring provinces of other sovereignties seriously hampered his work in his own enclave (p. 409). At this resistance beyond his control he was almost in despair until he noted that the times, in the person of the younger officials in these neighboring provinces, tended to favor him. However, it was clear that progress would be slow and at great cost (p. 410). So Odoard's condition as it refers to the ruling family, to his outlook in his enclave, to his own family, is discouraging. In "Das nußbraune Mädchen" Goethe took pains to show how the ideal marital relationship of the leaders Lenardo and Susanne had, by implication, a beneficial influence on the people of their group. In "Wer ist der Verräter?" something similar was to be noted. In "Die neue Melusine" a magical relation between the marriage of the princess and the well-being of the people was reported. Now conversely one wonders to what extent Odoard's unsatisfactory marriage will exert an unhappy influence on the well-being of the people of his province.

In considering the wife Albertina and her *Hausfreund*, it should not be forgotten that in a sense Odoard had set his wife a bad example with his devotion, unrequited, of course, to the Princess Sophronie in the Aurora affair. Still, it is clearly Goethe's intention to depict Albertina as the marriage partner most at fault. Of her he made the most damning remark of any character in the novel: "Albertine war eine von den Frauenzimmern, denen man unter vier Augen nichts zu sagen hätte, die man aber sehr gern in großer Gesellschaft sieht" (p. 402).† From the old woman it is learned further that Odoard has not taken a mistress, although a prospective one has been trying to catch his attention (pp. 395f), for which she praised his self-control.

If one goes outside the confines of the *Novelle* proper into the introductory and supplementary material, strong corroboration is to be found for the trends that have been observed within it. Just after Odoard finished telling his tale, the plans for the settlement in the new world were discussed: "[Wir legen] großes Gewicht auf die Familienkreise," (p. 405)‡ says Lenardo. "Den Hausvätern und Hausmüttern denken wir große Verpflichtungen zuzuteilen; die Erziehung wird bei uns um so leichter, *als jeder für sich selbst, Knecht und Magd, Diener und Dienerin*, stehen muß" (p. 405, italics added).* This makes an unhappy contrast with the family picture that one gets from Odoard's song, which glorified the leader (Odoard), and then addressed him as follows:

> Du verteilest Kraft und Bürde
> Und erwägst es ganz genau
> Gibst dem Alten Ruh und Würde
> Jünglingen Geschäft und Frau.
> Wechselseitiges Vertrauen
> Wird ein reinlich Häuschen bauen
> Schließen Hof- und Gartenzaun
> Auch der Nachbarschaft Vertrauen. (p. 413)§

---

† Albertina was one of those women to whom one would have nothing to say in a tête à tête, but whom one likes very much to see in a large social group.

‡ [We lay] great weight on family circles.

* We intend to distribute large responsibilities to the fathers and mothers of households; education is so much the easier with us, *since everyone must answer for himself, hired man and hired girl, and men and woman servants*.

> § You distribute power and burdens
> and consider it very carefully,
> (You) give the old men peace and dignity
> the younger men an occupation and a wife.
> Mutual trust
> will build a neat little house
> will join the fence of the courtyard and the garden
> to the trust of the neighborhood too.

This is not the sturdy independence of Lenardo's people; this is a kind of despotism, hopefully benevolent. It is also fitting that the song was not sung spontaneously, but to a popular tune from printed sheets that Odoard himself had passed out!

The contrast in the matter of leadership is also striking. In Lenardo's group, although they mistrust rule by the majority, authority is shared. The heads of family have considerable authority, and *Die Obrigkeit* (the authorities) is apparently a term that is widely inclusive. The controllers of the police rotate, and if necessary they have authority to call together *Geschworene* (a jury). In Odoard's area he alone had "unumschränkte Vollmacht" (complete, unlimited power), and to judge from the song that he had the group sing in his honor, he used it.

On the question of art there is another significant contrast. Lenardo's group has little to say about art in the new world, except "daß wir die Vorteile der Kultur mit hinübernehmen und die Nachteile zurücklassen. Branntweinschenken und Lesebibliotheken werden bei uns nicht geduldet" (p. 408).‡ But the Abbé, spokesman of the group, had said: "Die Künste sind das Salz der Erde; wie dieses zu den Speisen, so verhalten sich jene zu der Technik" (p. 242).* In Odoard's province there are bars ("Schenke," p. 413—there is no mention of lending libraries), but more important is his limited attitude towards the arts. On "die freien Künste" (literature, painting, etc.) he says "daß es ganz gleichgültig ist, ob sie gut oder schlecht getrieben werden" (p. 412).† In his view "die strengen Künste" (handicrafts) are more important. "Und doch hat jede [freie] Kunst ihre inneren Gesetze, deren Nichtbeobachtung aber der Menschheit keinen Schaden bringt, dagegen die strengen Künste dürfen sich nichts erlauben" (p. 412).§ This is in sharp contrast to the close interrelationship between the two which Wilhelm learned was desirable during his medical studies: "Es . . . sei zu bemerken, wie Kunst und Technik [die strengen Künste] sich

‡ that we will take across the advantages of culture and leave behind the disadvantages. We don't tolerate bars or lending libraries.
* The arts are the salt of the earth. As salt is to food, such is the relationship of [the arts] to technology.
† that it makes no difference, whether they are done well or badly.
§ And still every [free] art has its inner laws, the non-observance of which brings no harm to humanity; however, the handicrafts can't permit any liberties.

immer gleichsam die Waage halten und so nah verwandt immer eine zu der andern sich hinneigt, so daß die Kunst nicht sinken kann, ohne in löbliches Handwerk überzugehen, das Handwerk sich nicht steigern, ohne kunstreich zu werden" (p. 330).* Instead Odoardo's heavy emphasis on the crafts, coupled with seeming scorn for "die freien Künste," borders on a narrow-minded philistinism.

In the third and last book of the *Wanderjahre* Goethe placed three narrative insertions that are all negative examples, "Die neue Melusine," "Die gefährliche Wette" and "Nicht zu weit." To be sure, another narrative insertion follows, "Lenardos Tagebuch, Fortsetzung," but since that is really part III of "Das nußbraune Mädchen," which goes back to book I, it is of no present concern. It has already been noted that the negative example "Nicht zu weit" near the end of the novel is in purposeful contrast to "St. Joseph II" at the beginning, which is a model of what is good, healthy, and positive in marriage and family life. But in addition to that, "Nicht zu weit" is the summation or capstone, so to speak, of this final group of negative examples, since it combines the motivating themes of the preceding two.

In "Die neue Melusine" the nameless hero's chief failings are lack of self-control and lack of loyalty. Despite the explicit warnings before the fact by his beloved princess, and despite her repeated forgivenesses after the fact, the hero overindulged in wine, got into fights, and chased after strange women. In a climactic act of disloyalty at the end he deserted her, her (and his) unborn child and her dwarf world. In "Nicht zu weit" disloyalty is, if possible, raised to a more intense level. Odoard was disloyal to his wife Albertina in the affair with the princess Sophronie before the story opened, which affair at the very end seems about to be resumed. And then Albertina had, for some little time, been disloyal to her husband with her "Hausfreund".

In "Die gefährliche Wette" the dominant emotions of hate and anger aroused by the student prank broke up the group of students, endangered the narrator Christoph, hastened the death of the aris-

---

* Be it noted how art and technology [the strict arts] are always so to speak in balance, and so closely related one always inclines to the other, so art cannot sink without becoming laudable handicraft, and handicrafts cannot rise, without becoming artistic.

tocratic gentleman with the large nose and resulted in a scar which permanently disfigured Raufbold. In "Nicht zu weit" the anger and hate are all the keener for being between those who were formerly intimate: after the birthday-party fiasco Odoard specifically confessed his hate for Albertina. And then Goethe's description of Albertina's carriage ride wedged in with her deceivers makes it clear that here anger and hate are most intense.

Why should Goethe have wanted to put such a pessimistic note as this narrative insertion, "Nicht zu weit," with the accompanying materials from Odoard's speech and plans, near the end of the novel? The answer is connected with the fact that this tale is one of the new elements in the 1829 version. In the earlier form of the novel Goethe had adopted a quite different attitude toward emigration; Lenardo had expressed himself strongly against it, calling it "Grille, Wahn" (whim, delusion). In the final version it is, of course, the ideal. What "Nicht zu weit" represents in essence is a contrast to the league of emigrants, and, as has been seen, it is a gloomy and melancholy one. One must conclude then that sometime after 1821 Goethe's view of the future Germany and of Europe took on a much darker hue than it had previously. Hildebrandt attributes this to the poet's anger at Metternich's policies.[10]

On three occasions here toward the end of the novel Goethe has tried to depict the life of those who will remain behind in Europe. Susanne's old *Gehilfe*, new brother-in-law to the *Geschirrfasser*, plans to set up mechanical looms in the mountain valleys. There is one reference to a more promising future, but there still persists the melancholy impression left by the ominous phrase noted above, that the machine operators are going "die Nahrung der Menge an sich zu reißen" (p. 430).† Then secondly Goethe had shown those members of the emigrating group who had failed at the last minute as *Entsagende*, so to speak, because of incautious love affairs—they had gotten their girlfriends pregnant—and how that group was used by the *Amtmann*.[11] Again the picture is a discouraging one of a group held together by unhappy social and economic needs, and exploited by clever and scheming men of business. Lastly and most discouragingly, in "Nicht zu weit" the author shows how undesirable in essence conditions in Europe really were by showing the flagrant

† to snatch for themselves the people's livelihood.

discrepancies between them and the ideal of the family as *Urform* and *Metamorphose*, despite the seeming advantages that Odoard enjoyed in his unhindered power and in his isolated province. What this means, then, as has been demonstrated by applying the yardstick of the family as *Urform* and *Metamorphose* to the succeeding elements of the novel, is that as of 1829 Goethe had come to realize, and here expressed his realization in symbolic form, that the outlook for the future seemed far more promising in the new world than it did in the old.

In conclusion then the series of titled narrative insertions in the *Wanderjahre* demonstrate something vital about the forms of human association, from the positive model "St. Joseph II" to the negative model of "Nicht zu weit," with a variety of intermediate positions. The insertions deal furthermore with the same subject matter as the main plot and in fact bring it to a series of illustrative instances that define important aspects of the family as *Urform* and *Metamorphose* of society. Thus the parts, though numerous and diverse, are still bound to each other and to the main plot in essential ways that reinforce the unity of the whole.

XIII
THE NONTITLED NARRATIVE INSERTIONS

TWO OF THESE have already been dealt with under the title "Wilhelm's Prehistory" ("Die Fischerknaben," "Wilhelm's Medical Education"). These were taken out of order because of their similarity to the three-fold history of Lenardo's love affair: "Das nußbraune Mädchen" and "Lenardo's Tagebuch I und II." Earlier there was occasion to quote the views of some critics to the effect that the main plot of the novel contains, in addition to the novellas, other almost independent narrative elements, among which were mentioned Makarie, "Die pädagogische Provinz" and the scenes at the Lago Maggiore.[1] For the purpose of the present investigation, two more will be examined, "Berggespräche mit Montan" (Mountain conversations with Montan), and the *Amtmann* (steward) and his labor force. There are, of course, others, for instance, the uncle, his history and estate, the old collector, and so on. However, it is confidently expected that the examination of the five listed above will produce a method which can be used to deal satisfactorily with the remainder. These five will be looked at then to determine to what extent Goethe treated them comparably to or differently from the titled narrative insertions.

"BERGGESPRÄCHE MIT MONTAN I UND II" (MOUNTAIN CONVERSATIONS WITH MONTAN I AND II)

When Wilhelm heard at "Saint" Joseph's that Montan was nearby, he resolved to search out his old friend from the *Lehrjahre*, known there as Jarno. He was guided to Jarno's mountaintop by the doubtful urchin Fitz (p. 3), and at the end he was guided down by a *Bote*. If one looks ahead to the *Berggespräch II*, one finds that that too takes place on a mountain top (p. 259), and that Wilhelm had to be guided there also. Thus it becomes apparent that Goethe here is using two techniques to set off these conversations between old friends: first the geographical limitation of the mountain peaks and secondly the "frame" of having Wilhelm guided up (and down). Notable also is that as Wilhelm approaches the summit where Montan is, the latter reaches down and gives him a powerful lift upward, symbolic of the relationship he has had to Wilhelm from the first, that of an older and wiser friend lending a helping hand. On arriving at the top, Wilhelm looked out over the tremendous view of mountains, foot hills and low-lands stretching far away (it has been suggested that these symbolize the entire "life" that Wilhelm is about to enter into in the novel to come) and promptly got a dizzy spell. Montan reassured him: ". . . es ist nichts natürlicher, als daß uns vor einem großen Anblick schwindelt. Aber es ist überhaupt kein echter Genuß, als da, wo man erst schwindeln muß" (p. 31).*

Nearly everything at these rarefied heights is symbolic. Montan lectured Felix, for instance: ". . . so merke dir, daß du gegenwärtig auf dem ältesten Gebirge, auf dem frühesten Gestein dieser Welt sitzest" (p. 31).† The type of stone wasn't identified until later (p. 42), but it was granite. And for Goethe the pantheist and skilled geologist, contact with the granite mountain top guaranteed direct contact with the essence of the earth and hence with nature; here insights came more quickly and easily, here truth was more nearly approachable. In his 1784 essay "Über den Granit" Goethe had called the stone the core of the earth (13.254) and "der älteste, tiefste, unerschütterlichste Sohn der Natur" (the oldest, deepest, most unshakable son of nature, 13.255). Sitting on a granite peak he wrote:

In diesem Augenblicke, da die innern anziehenden und bewegenden Kräfte der Erde gleichsam unmittelbar auf mich wirken, da die Einflüsse des Himmels mich näher umschweben, werde ich zu höhere Betrachtungen der

---

* . . . there is nothing more natural than that we should get dizzy before a great outlook. But in general there is no genuine pleasure except where one must first feel dizzy.

† . . . so remember that you are now sitting on the oldest mountains, on the earliest rock type of this world.

Natur hinaufgestimmt, und wie der Menschengeist alles belebt, so wird auch ein Gleichnis in mir rege, dessen Erhabenheit ich nicht widerstehen kann. (13.255)‡

In the opening pages of the novel, also up here on the mountain heights, a symbolic conversation had taken place. Felix had found an interesting rock:

"Wie nennt man diesen Stein, Vater?" sagte der Knabe.
"Ich weiß nicht," versetzte Wilhelm.
"Ist das wohl Gold, was darin so glänzt?" sagte jener.
"Es ist keins," versetzte dieser, "und ich erinnere mich, daß die Leute es Katzengold nenne."
"Katzengold!" sagte der Knabe lächelnd, "und warum?"
"Wahrscheinlich weil es falsch ist und man die Katzen auch für falsch hält." (p. 4)*

In other words, Wilhelm symbolically faces a problem every parent must, first how to answer the endless questions of, and then how to educate, his offspring. In the ensuing exchanges with Montan it is clear that this is uppermost in his mind. The problem is to stay with him through "die pädagogische Provinz" clear to the last scene of the novel. It is the wise Montan who makes the pithy assertions up here; "In every new circle one must begin anew, as a child would" (p. 33); "Beginnings are easy, it is the ending that is much harder" (p. 36). The reader then hears that one must serve from the bottom up, that it is best to restrict oneself to a craft. And then: "Mache ein Organ aus dir und erwarte, was für eine Stelle dir die Menschheit im allgemeinen Leben wohlmeinend zugestehen werde" (p. 37).† Montan says further that the days of the well-rounded education are past,

---

‡ In this moment, as the inner attracting and moving forces of the earth, so to speak, influence me, when the influences of the heavens hover closer about me, my mood is lifted to higher observations of nature, and as the human spirit enlivens everything, so a simile becomes active in me, a simile the sublimity of which I cannot withstand.

* "What's this stone called, father?" said the boy.
"I don't know," responded Wilhelm.
"Is that gold, do you suppose, that's gleaming in it?" said the former.
"No, it's not," responded the latter, "and I remember that people call it cat's gold [fool's gold]."
"Cat's gold," said the boy smiling, "and why?"
"Probably because it is false [or deceitful] and people think cats are deceitful too."

† Make yourself into an organic element [of the whole] and wait and see what kind of a position humanity will benevolently assign you in life.

and that "jetzo ist die Zeit der Einseitigkeiten" (now is the age of specializations, p. 37) and recommends a trade. But Wilhelm is not sure: "Ich möchte aber doch . . . meinem Sohn einen freieren Blick über die Welt verschaffen, als ein beschränktes Handwerk zu geben vermag. Man umgrenze den Menschen, wie man wolle, so schaut er doch in seiner Zeit umher; und wie kann er begreifen, wenn er nicht einigermaßen weiß, was vorhergegangen ist" (p. 39).‡

The two friends now adjourned to the hut and the kiln of a charcoal burner, when Montan referred to the smoldering kiln as "an excellent educational institution" (p. 39). He explained how the charcoal burner, after lighting the fire, banked it with earth so that it would not burn wildly and fiercely but must smolder under control until all the wood had been turned into the desired charcoal. Montan then proudly called himself "an old basket of good beechwood charcoal" (p. 40). It was he who first impressed on Wilhelm the need to renounce (p. 33); how he meant the reference to himself as charcoal needs some explanation. In the *Lehrjahre* the reader got to know Jarno as the natural son of a prince, that is to say, as a man whose birth guaranteed him wealth and position. Under the *ancien régime* of the eighteenth century no man with his advantages would have deserted society to devote himself to the study of mountains and rocks, which Jarno-Montan has done, "in order not to become a misanthropist" (p. 444). The reader is apparently to understand that the enormous social upheaval of the French Revolution has occurred between the *Lehrjahre* and the *Wanderjahre*. As a result Montan lost wealth, position, and influence and, angry at the world of men, he fled to the silent world of mountains and rocks. By comparing himself to beechwood charcoal he apparently meant that he hadn't permitted his natural rage, resentment, and bitterness to flare fiercely and burn himself out, so to speak, but instead had directed and controlled the fiery energies of his bitterness to mastering his new profession of geology.

During the conversation Wilhelm drew a *Besteck* (case of instruments) out of his pocket, which Montan recognized. Only later does

‡ I should like, however, . . . to give my son a freer view of the world than a limited handicraft can give. You can limit the human being as much as you want, still he will look around in his own time, and how can he understand [it] if he doesn't know at least to a certain extent what went before.

the reader learn that the instruments were chirurgical ones, which means that Wilhelm was planning to devote his life to medicine. However, the act was also symbolic, for it was a transition: the two friends had begun their all-night conversation with the question of Felix's education, and now Montan has referred to his own profession. Wilhelm's consideration of the *Besteck* marks his shift of attention to his own professional plans, conversations that will continue on the professional level in *Berggespräch II*. In the 1821 version Goethe had quite appropriately had Montan recommend to Wilhelm the pedagogical province as a suitable place for Felix's further education.[2] In the final version it was Lenardo who did so. The only obvious reason for the change is that perhaps Lenardo would have been better acquainted with the contemporary world than the semi-hermit Montan.

There are several interesting features about the second conversation. First of all it is framed by editorial comment (pp. 258 and 264). Secondly, the two visits to the pedagogical province and the two mountaintop conversations with Montan come to a climax together, which is appropriate, since they all concern educational problems. Most interesting of all is the spectacular symbolic use of light. As Wilhelm climbed towards the rendezvous in the evening, suddenly torches were lit and he saw over the whole side of the mountain long lines of light converging at the top. On arrival the concentrated lights illuminated the summit brilliantly, and there the long conversations on the origin of the earth took place (pp. 260–61). It is the old simile, as old as Sophocles' *Oedipus* and older; light equates with knowledge, darkness with ignorance. And at the end Montan gave the essence of his wisdom: "Denken und Tun, Tun und Denken, das ist die Summe aller Weisheit" (p. 263).*
Thought is necessary, but needs to be tried out in action, and action is needed, but should be tested continually by thought. And he concluded that the old miner's greeting, *Glück auf!* (Luck is the thing!), important as luck is, should be changed to *Sinn auf!* (Sense [or intelligence] is the thing!).

The parallels here are important. In *Berggespräch I* the main subject was the education of children, particularly Felix. In the second it is Montan's professional development. In the first "the fire" of moti-

---

* Thinking and acting, acting and thinking, that is the sum of all wisdom.

THE NONTITLED NARRATIVE INSERTIONS   99

vation that Montan applied first to himself and then to others was the *Kohlenmeiler*, in the second it is the dazzling (torch-) light of knowledge.

And the reader sees a metamorphosis of the *Urform* family at work here as in the novellas, but this time as education, in a quite new fashion. Hegel, in his *Philosophy of Law*, had distinguished three phases in the family: the marriage, family property and capital, and the third was the education of the children.

"DIE PÄDAGOGISCHE PROVINZ"

Book II, chapters 1, 2, 8, and 9, are probably the most discussed and analyzed of the entire work, first because they deal with pedagogy, which from the first was a central theme of the *Wilhelm Meister* novels, and secondly because the subject matter is not only important and of widespread interest, but also because Goethe's ideas were anything but conventional for the time. Almost everyone who has written on the *Wanderjahre* has had something to say about the *Provinz*. Of the specific literature on that alone, the studies by Kohlmeyer, Jungmann, Beutler, Jantz, Flitner and Ohly are to be recommended.[3] However, my intent will not be to investigate the educational philosophy involved, nor the sources Goethe may have used; this has been done and there is no need to repeat. Instead the goal will be to examine how the author attached the material to the novel and whether signs of the family or its metamophoses are to be identified.

In one way, the *Provinz* forms a sort of transition into this category of untitled narrative insertions; the author does not set off the title on the printed page as he did, say, with "Wer ist der Verräter?," but he does give the reader in the text the phrase by which to identify these sketches (p. 244). When Wilhelm and Felix enter the area, they cross a border (p. 149), as does Wilhelm alone when he leaves (p. 166), which confirms the fact that there is again a frame, a geographical one this time. But it soon becomes evident that Wilhelm, in seeking the leaders, crosses several concentric boundaries. He passes through a landscape of agricultural lands and is led into a *Talwald* (literally, a valleywood) through a gate in a wall.

Then he comes into a building where he is greeted by the leaders and then shown some explanatory and educational paintings in a gallery. An outer gallery here contains scenes from the Old Testament, an inner one pictures from the New Testament, the crucifixion excepted. Depictions of that are in an inner sanctum, "Das Heiligtum des Schmerzes" (the sanctuary of pain), which are not shown to Wilhelm. Exactly how many barriers there are depends on how one counts, but it is plain that Goethe here used the physical and geographical space to set these elements off from the main plot.

In describing the Old Testament gallery Wilhelm's guide used language that was startling in its applicability not only to the Old Testament but also to the complex form of the *Wanderjahre* that has been observed so far.

> Ein Hauptvorteil . . . ist die treffliche Sammlung ihrer heiligen Bücher. Sie stehen so glücklich beisammen, daß aus den fremdesten Elementen ein täuschendes Ganze entgegentritt. Sie sind vollständig genug, um zu befriedigen, fragmentarisch genug um anzureizen; hinlänglich barbarisch, um aufzufordern, hinlänglich zart, um zu besänftigen. (p. 160)†

In the second of the two portions that deal with the *Provinz* (chapters 8 and 9), one again finds editorial comments that function as a frame. The *Zwischenrede* (intermediate comment) specifies the passing of a "few years" (p. 240). Then at the end there is a comment (p. 264) which ends this part and leads into the next. The frame is also identifiable roughly in the middle of the section, as Goethe, under the guise of the *Redakteur* (editor) comments on the antitheater attitudes of the authorities of the *Provinz* (p. 258).

Furthermore, each area of Wilhelm's visit to the *Provinz* is carefully outlined. First he entered a flat landscape where horses were raised (p. 244), then an area with low, green hills, where musicians were trained (p. 247). The architects were to be found in a city (p. 249), as were apparently the other artists (pp. 252–56). Finally on the summit of the mountains he again met his old friend Montan. In other words, in *Provinz I* and *II* Goethe used not only the frame

---

† A main advantage . . . is the excellent collection of their holy books. They fit so fortunately together that a deceptive unity appears out of the most disparate elements. They are complete enough to be satisfying, fragmentary enough to be stimulating, sufficiently barbaric to be challenging, sufficiently delicate to calm one.

technique, but also a careful delineation of the immediate landscape to set the material off from the main plot. And he used the space described to emphasize the subject matter dealt with: in *Provinz I* Wilhelm had to penetrate several barriers on his way to an understanding of the concentric circles of meaning. Toward the end of *Provinz II* the concentration of lights at the top of the mountain brilliantly illuminated, literally and figuratively, the old friends and their conversation. Here, with musical enhancement, the climactic conversations on the origin of the earth and on "Tun und Denken" took place.

At first glance there seems to be little about the family in the *Provinz*, at least not in the way it has been seen so far. However, it will be recalled that Hegel's *Philosophy of Law* specifically included education as a part of the responsibility of the family, and Goethe knew Hegel. Furthermore there are metamorphoses of the family in which the members do not need to be blood related—a group gathered for a common purpose can be so considered. Thus the students and their instructors at the *Provinz* could be a "family." And there is yet another aspect to be considered. There is no question but that Philipp Emmanuel von Fellenberg's institution at Hofwyl near Bern in Switzerland was in many respects Goethe's model for the *Provinz*, and Goethe had had direct contact with the leaders of the school. One of the letters from Fellenberg to Goethe said:

> Unser großes deutsches Vaterland bedarf eines Platzes, auf dem die Kinder der entzweiten Väter aus Preußen, Bayern, Österreich usw. zur Eintracht und zu den gemeinschaftlichen würdigen Bestrebungen für das allgemeine Beste, deren wir so sehr bedürfen, erzogen werden können.
>
> Alle diese Zwecke hoffe ich durch eine sorgfältige Konstituirung einer pädagogischen Republik erreicht zu sehen.‡ [4]

In *Provinz II* there are indications that Goethe also saw the educational activities as linked to the larger German populace, the *Volk*, the larger metamorphosis of the family, as was seen among the mountain weavers of *Lenardos Tagebuch*. Son Felix and his contem-

‡ Our great German fatherland needs a place in which the children of the separated fathers from Prussia, Bavaria, Austria, etc., can be educated for harmony and for the worthy common aims for the general well-being that we all need so much.

I hope to see all these aims attained by means of the careful founding of a pedagogical republic.

poraries raise horses for an annual market, "das große Marktfest," to which buyers came from all the provinces (the poetic plural, *Lande*, not *Länder*, is used, hence presumably these are provinces of Germany), and from foreign countries as well (p. 245). Among the musicians cooperation of large groups was emphasized (p. 247), and finally the work of the architects was described thus: "Sie müssen sich zuletzt dergestalt über das Gemeine erheben, daß die ganze Volksgemeinde in und an ihren Werken sich veredelt fühle" (p. 251).* One of the arts would seem to be made in order to influence wider circles of the populace, namely the theater, but it is just this that was decried and banned from the *Provinz* (p. 256).

MAKARIE

It may seem strange that this investigation now turns to Makarie without first considering her brother, the uncle from America, his history, his home, and his family. It was through him that Wilhelm met Makarie, and he seems well suited for present purposes. He lived on an estate cut off from the rest of the countryside; since he owned the land in America to which the emigrants plan to go he was a man of key importance, and his family becomes the most important in the novel. However, from early in the novel (p. 64) two of his family, Hersilie and Lenardo, become full participating members of the main plot, and so his domain and family, for present purposes, are not considered a narrative insertion. Where to draw the line between the main plot and the insertions has caused problems for other commentators. Klingenberg, for instance, excludes both "St. Joseph II" and "Der Mann von funfzig Jahren" from her list of novellas on the grounds that they are both part of the main plot. Both she and the present study are, for convenience of analysis, making distinctions that, as will be demonstrated later, Goethe probably did not make. At the end of this section there will be occasion to return to this problem and, it is to be hoped, propose a solution to explain everything satisfactorily. In the meantime, how-

---

* They must finally raise themselves above the common level that the whole folk-community may feel itself ennobled in and at the sight of their works.

ever, the section on the uncle will not be treated as a narrative insertion.

On approaching Makarie's estate, Wilhelm and Felix had to go through a gate in a wall into an enclosed space before they could attain the residence itself. Once inside, in a large room, Makarie appeared in a wheel chair from behind a green curtain. One is reminded of the concentric barriers Wilhelm had to penetrate to get to the core of the *Provinz*—here as there the external locality sets off the material described. The area around Makarie is further set off in that no horses are permitted on the estate. Horses are strong and brutish, while Makarie's area is the center of the intellect, of the mind.[5]

During his first conversation with the lady in the wheel chair, Wilhelm noted the collection of pedagogical paintings on the walls (p. 115). This is one of several such series: the uncle's castle (p. 79); in "Wer ist der Verräter?" (p. 101); the pedagogical province (p. 158), "Der Mann von funfzig Jahren" (p. 179); the Lago Maggiore (p. 227); all of which taken together show the very high regard Goethe held for the moral and pedagogical value of plastic art.

Previously Wilhelm had learned to know several people from Makarie's circle, both personally and from letters. Here one of Makarie's most significant human attributes shone through to him: she saw and could describe people with matchless penetration and clarity.

... es war als wenn sie die innere Natur eines jeden durch die ihn umgebende individuelle Maske durchschaute. Die Personen, welche Wilhelm kannte, standen wie verklärt vor seiner Seele, das einsichtige Wohlwollen der unschätzbaren Frau hatte die Schale losgelöst und den gesunden Kern veredelt und belebt. (p. 116)†

This is the quality for which Makarie was chiefly revered by family and intimates.

When, then, Wilhelm got into a conversation on mathematics with Makarie's companion and resident scholar, the astronomer, the

† ... it was as if she saw through into the inner nature of everyone, through the individual mask that surrounded him. The people Wilhelm knew stood transfigured before his soul, the insightful good will of the incomparable woman had cleared away the shell and ennobled and enlivened the healthy kernel.

latter began to read a paper on mathematics which, however, was *not* included in the novel. Instead the editor broke in as follows:

Unsere Freunde haben einen Roman in die Hand genommen, und wenn dieser hie und da schon mehr als billig didaktisch geworden so finden wir doch geraten, die Geduld unserer Wohlwollenden nicht noch weiter auf die Probe zu stellen. Die Papiere, die uns vorliegen, gedenken wir an einen anderen Orte abdrucken zu lassen und fahren diesmal im Geschichtlichen ohne weiteres fort, da wir selbst ungeduldig sind, das obwaltende Rätsel aufgeklärt zu sehen. (p. 118)‡

Here Goethe not only admitted to being perhaps too didactic, but he also mistrusts the capacity of the reader to absorb the material! Then follows another unreported conversation, but Wilhelm summarized this one: "Große Gedanken und ein reines Herz, das ist's, was wir uns von Gott erbitten sollten!" (p. 118).* This latter is of course an aphorism, to which we shall have cause to return. Angela took him to a room where many manuscripts were kept, including notebooks full of pithy summaries of conversations (aphorisms), similar to the one he himself had just made (pp. 124–25). This is Makarie's archive, and the notebooks contain the aphorisms that will be considered in greater detail later.

In Makarie's house Wilhelm then had the dream or vision that informs him clearly about his own future, a vision that has already been referred to: ". . . meine Absicht ist, einen edlen Familienkreis in allen seinen Gliedern erwünscht verbunden herzustellen" (p. 119).† And then he mounted the observatory tower and observed a symbol of all the heavenly bodies, Jupiter, which was after all named for the father of the Greek family of the gods, and which planet is surrounded by moons, as if to symbolize a family.

Finally with Angela (note the name—most of Goethe's names are meaningful), Makarie's female assistant, he inspected the girls' school that Makarie conducted on her estate, which demonstrated

‡ Our friends [the readers] have taken a novel into their hands, and if the latter here and there has gotten a little more didactic than reasonable, still we find it advisable not to put the patience of our well-wishers even further to the test. We intend to print the papers that lie before us in another place, and we continue in the narrative without further ado, since we ourselves are impatient to see the prevailing puzzle cleared up.

* Great thoughts and a pure heart, that is what we should ask for from God!

† . . . it is my intention to produce a noble family circle bound together as one would wish in all its members.

the lady's family sense of responsibility for the education of the rising generation, themselves future mothers of families.

In what might be called Makarie II, the second place in the novel where the attention is focused on her (Book III, chapters 14 and 15), chapter 15 is devoted to the vision of Makarie as part of the solar system, where the human and the scientific form a mystical union. Chapter 14 is, so to speak, the climax or zenith of the various family plot-developments of the novel. Here the reader finds a description of the various families that have been formed or are forming around Makarie as they all assemble on her estate before going either to America (the league of emigrants) or back to their own possessions (the Major, the beautiful widow, Flavio, and Hilarie).

The influence of this secular saint on her friends is of vital importance and often leads their development to a sudden and higher plateau, to a *Steigerung* (enhancement) in the Goethean sense, of their essential character. Wilhelm underwent such an inner transformation to a higher state in his insight, quoted in the preceding paragraphs, about his future mission in life. After the "end" of "Der Mann von funfzig Jahren," the beautiful widow, deeply dissatisfied with herself, had turned to Makarie, "die Vertraute, der Beichtiger aller bedrängter Seelen, aller derer, die sich selbst verloren haben, sich wiederzufinden wünschten und nicht wissen wo" (p. 223).‡ The secular saint Makarie "im Vorhalten eines sittlich-magischen Spiegels, durch die äußere verworrene Gestalt irgendeinem Unglücklichen sein rein schönes Innere gewiesen und ihn auf einmal erst mit sich selbst befriedigt und zu einem neuen Leben aufgefordert hat" (p. 223).* Without direct contact with Makarie, only through correspondence, the beautiful widow had been led to a higher potentiality of character; Makarie had caused a *Steigerung*. Similarly for Wilhelm also Makarie's mere nearness (she was not actually present) was enough to cause the *Steigerung*. Finally it will be recalled that in chapter 14 of Book III a number of marriages and engagements are announced at Makarie's estate. How many of these

‡ the confidante, the confessor of all oppressed souls, of all those who have lost themselves, who would like to find themselves again and don't know where.

* by holding in front [of them] a moral-magical mirror, showed some unhappy person his own beautiful, pure essence through the confused external features and suddenly for the first time has [made him] satisfied with himself and has challenged him to a new life.

were due to a *Steigerung* brought about by Makarie's influence is not clear, possibly those of Philine and Lydie.

LAGO MAGGIORE

After leaving the pedagogical province Wilhelm had a pious pilgrimage to make; he had apparently promised himself to visit the home country of the child Mignon, to whom he had become so attached in the *Lehrjahre*. It is the area of the Lago Maggiore at first, and then the actual body of water itself, that becomes the frame for these pages of the novel. On the way thither he met a painter who was also enamoured of the memory of Mignon (about whom he had only read in the *Lehrjahre*!), and together they sought out her old home, and then crisscrossed the lake by boat.[6]

Here they met the two ladies from the novella "Der Mann von funfzig Jahren," the beautiful widow and Hilarie, and for several days there ensued a strange sort of contact on water by day and a separation on land by night (pp. 232f), due to Wilhelm's oath not to spend more than three days at one place. Here by day in boats on the lake they pursued art projects and remembered Mignon with great sentiment. Finally they spent three days together on the Isola Bella (Beautiful Island) in the middle of the lake. Of obvious importance in this story by the lake was the role that art played. Goethe described with loving care the individual sheets from the portfolios of the painter, which showed (pp. 235f) the various stages of Mignon's story. More important was the development of Hilarie's artistic gifts under the tutelage of the painter; from a gifted amateur she blossomed into a skilled artist in these few days. The "sittliche Nachwirkung" (moral after-effect) was crucial—art helped her come to terms with her own emotional problems.

The blossoming that Hilarie here experiences is important from another point of view; it is only the third clear example of a *Steigerung* (enhancement) of character to be found in the novel (the others were in the vicinity of Makarie). Hilarie had always had artistic talent as a pianist and poetess, or at least versifier, in addition to her accomplishments in drawing. In these few days by the lake, whether because of the beautiful surroundings, whether because of the congenial society, whether because of the skilled instruction of Wilhelm's friend the painter, or whether because of a combination of all of these, Hilarie underwent a *Steigerung* of character and personality that not only turned her into a skilled artist but also enabled her to come to terms with her previous emotional problems.

Just as important was the fact that all four of them who either already belonged to the league of renunciants or who soon joined it, remained true to their original loves; Wilhelm to Natalie, the widow to the Major, and Hilarie, although she had not yet formally accepted him, to Flavio. Despite the fact that they were all young and beautiful, despite the fact that they had been in close proximity for some days, despite the fact that they had been dealing with emotional subjects like art and Mignon's memory, no new, confusing cross-attractions blossomed, although apparently some might have. On the last day the ladies departed at daybreak without a farewell, forbidding the men to follow them, in what looks like a flight. Such constancy proves them fit, of course, to enter into proper family relationships.

THE *AMTMANN* AND HIS LABOR FORCE

Near the very end of the novel (Book III, chapter 16), the castle that had held the now-departed emigrant group seemed deserted. The *Amtmann* (steward) was still there, however, with a few occupants. They were a group that had planned to join either Lenardo's party or Odoard's, but who had, so to speak, failed their first test. These were young men who had "[sich] mehr oder weniger befreundet" (more or less made friends, 453) with some village girls, whom they had gotten pregnant, to which situation Goethe humorously refers as "ein bürgerlicher Unfall" (a civil accident, p. 454). Such an "accident" would, of course, disqualify them as *Entsagende* (renunciants). Since they could not emigrate and needed to remain behind, the *Amtmann* set up a furniture factory to exploit the unexpected labor supply. There are dark elements here: it is clear that the marriages were anything but ideal, and in addition the *Amtmann* is referred to in ambiguous terms. When he first heard of the situation he "lachte heimlich als wahrer Egoist" (laughed secretly as true egoist, p. 454);

he determined "Nutzen [davon] zu ziehen" (to profit [from it], p. 453). Later he was referred to as "der gewandte Geschäftsman" (the skilled man of affairs, p. 454), and called "unsern rechnenden und berechnenden Geschäftsmann" (our computing and calculating man of business, p. 455). In other words, he was a capitalist, comparable to the *Geschirrfasser* who, with the *Gehülfe*, planned to bring machines into the mountain valleys. As has been seen, the latter two schemed to profit from the troubles of others. The *Amtmann* in a comparable way schemed to profit likewise. If one then contrasts these two leaders of economic groups with Susanne's work as factor, with the family as *Urform* and *Metamorphose* of human society as it is to be seen unfolding in this novel, then it becomes clear that despite the camouflage of ribald humor that Goethe inserted between the reader and the subject matter, the author was really condemning the *Amtmann* and his project. Here at the very end, then, Goethe is inserting another negative example that must be considered along with Odoard's "Nicht zu weit."[7]

In conclusion, then, it can be said that two things have become apparent about these various nontitled narrative insertions; firstly that whereas in the titled narrative insertions the plot plays a central role, in the nontitled ones it is much less important, and in two is almost nonexistent. Here the emphasis has been sharply shifted to the report of a conversation or conversations. The second factor of importance is that Goethe has made little or no distinction between the titled and the nontitled insertions in the method of setting them off from the rest of the material. They are all treated as separate units within the whole, principally by use of the frame.

The problem of what is and what is not to be considered as a narrative insertion is peculiarly difficult in this novel. As has been noted, the main plot contains several elements that are like novellas.[8] In each of the five untitled insertions chosen to be treated separately here there is some element, either a kind of sub-plot or the use of the frame, or both, to show that Goethe considered the insertion as a more or less separate entity.

From another point of view the entire novel can be considered as a typically Goethean series in which the narrative elements range from mere episodes within the main plot, for instance Wilhelm's visit to the *Sammler*, to completely independent *Novellen*, such as "Wer ist der Verräter?" Some are quite short, such as the *Amtmann's* labor force; others, like "Der Mann von funfzig Jahren," are very long. It is easy to separate the titled from the untitled narrative insertions, although "Die Fischerknaben" offers some problems. It is harder to make a distinction between a nontitled narrative insertion and a mere episode in the main plot, as for instance the estate of the uncle from America or the *Sammler*. However, precisely where one draws the line is not too important, as long as one is aware that one is examining a continuum of narrative elements, of which both the parts and the whole were carefully constructed by the author.

In other words Goethe makes no essential distinction between the titled and the nontitled insertions, between those that are obviously a part of the main plot and those that are not. In both categories is to be found the use of geographical limitations as a frame, and the frame is employed profusely otherwise. One finds everywhere the use of parallels and contrasts to other parts of the novel. Here as well as there the author uses aphorisms, and in addition shows a marked preference for the family as *Urform und Metamorphose*, as well as for the didactic use of collections of paintings. Thus it is evident that Goethe made no clear distinction between his types of narrative insertions, whether titled or nontitled, whether part of the central plot or off to one side. Since he treated them all more or less alike, the commentators should proceed similarly.

XIV
APHORISMS, MAXIMS AND REFLECTIONS

GOETHE'S ORIGINAL PLAN was to print the collection of aphorisms entitled "Aus Makariens Archiv" at the end of Book I, and the other collection, "Betrachtungen im Sinne der Wanderer" ("Reflections according to the Travelers") at the end of Book II, which is where they are shown in the schematic outline appended to this study (see pp. 144–45). The present displacement of "Aus Makariens Archiv" to the end of Book III follows the example of the printing of the only edition that occurred in Goethe's lifetime, "Die Ausgabe Letzter Hand," where the mistake arose first from Goethe's misunderstanding of the printer's schedule. He then gave a superficial reason for agreeing to the displaced position of printing which Eckermann then in turn misunderstood, so that after Goethe's death he removed the two collections completely from the new editions of the *Wanderjahre*. Wundt has demonstrated Eckermann's error,[1] and Trunz, who restored the collections to the place they held in the only edition to appear in Goethe's lifetime, has a good summary of the affair (pp. 682f and 718–20). He also wrote a careful account of how Goethe wrote the final version in 1828/29,[2] from which it is abundantly evident that the author took the composition and arrangement of the aphorism collections quite seriously, and that Eckermann's recollections are faulty.

Before proceeding with the collections, another question must be dealt with: the aphorisms are, to be sure, insertions, but to what extent can they be considered narrative insertions? An answer to this must be made in parts, and so a final justification needs to be held in abeyance for a short time. First it is in order to confirm or deny Stöcklein's assertion: "Die beiden größten Aphorismenketten sind den *Wanderjahren* äußerlich und innerlich eingebaut."*³ Even a cursory examination of the text shows repeated examples of general or generalizing statements that are close to aphorisms or maxims. Herewith a few random samples from this series:

Book I   pp. 36–37   Montans Berggespräch—contains many
          p. 65f   Uncle's castle—posted everywhere
          p. 123   Aphorism are kernels of conversations
          p. 148   "Handwerk in der Beschränkung erworben" (craft to be learned only in restricted circumstances)

Book II   pp. 151–60   Many from the *Provinz*
          p. 170   "Sein und Schein" (being and appearing)
          p. 206   "Dichtkunst als Heilmittel (poetry as therapeutic remedy)
          p. 218   "Später Mond und Liebe des Alters" (Late moon and love of old age)
          p. 242   "Kunst Salz der Erde" (art salt of the earth)
          p. 263   "Tun und Denken" (doing and thinking)
          pp. 268–83   "Die Fischerknaben"—contains many

Book III   p. 334   "Grundgesetz unserer Verbindung" (constitution of our league)
          p. 404   "Mensch muß sich ins Unvermeidliche fügen" (Man has to submit to the inevitable)
          p. 426   "Pflicht des Tages" (Duty of the day)
          p. 428   "Bei Makarie zeigt sich jeder wie er ist" (Near Makarie everyone shows in his true light)

It is unnecessary to cite any more; dozens of additional examples can be found at will. Such general and didactic language is indeed a pervasive characteristic of the novel.

Some of these aphorisms are conceived of as kernels of conversations. At Makarie's estate Angela reported:

Meine Herrin . . . ist von der Wichtigkeit des augenblicklichen Gesprächs höchlich überzeugt; dabei gehe vorüber, sagt sie, was kein Buch enthält,

---

* The two largest chains of aphorisms are externally and internally built into the *Wanderjahre*.

und doch wieder das Beste, was Bücher jemals enthalten haben. Deshalb machte sie mir's zur Pflicht, einzelne gute Gedanken aufzubewahren, die aus einem geistreichen Gespräch, wie Samenkörner aus einer vielästigen Pflanze, hervorspringen. (p. 123)†

Then Angela continues "dem Gaste wieder zu vertrauen, daß dadurch ein bedeutendes Archiv entstanden sei, woraus sie in schlaflosen Nächten manchmal ein Blatt Makarien vorlese" (p. 124).‡ Similarly, at the pedagogical province Wilhelm got into a conversation with the leaders: ". . . sein freundlicher Empfang von den Dreien, die sich nach und nach herbeifanden, löste sich endlich in ein Gespräch auf, wo jeder das Seinige beitrug, dessen Inhalt wir jedoch in der Kürze zusammenfassen" (p. 154).* Later the emigrant group around Lenardo got into conversation on which Friedrich took notes: "Indessen dürfen wir uns so lange nicht aufhalten und geben lieber gleich die Resultate, als daß wir uns verpflichteten, sie erst nach und nach in dem Geiste unserer Leser hervortreten zu lassen. Folgendes ergab sich als das Quintessenz dessen, was verhandelt wurde" (p. 404).§ It should not be overlooked that Goethe had for years been in the habit of looking on maxims and reflections as the kernels of conversations. In *Die Wahlverwandtschaften* he introduced the fifth segment of Ottilie's *Tagebuch* (Journal)—which consisted of her collection of aphorisms—thus: "Dieser Vorfall mag jedoch zu einem Gespräch Anlaß gegeben haben, wovon wir die Spuren in Ottiliens Tagebuch finden" (6.415).¶ Reiss sees the use of the aphorisms as "die Erweiterung des Erzähl- und Gedankenkomplexes" (the broadening of the complex of narrative and of

---

† My mistress . . . is completely convinced of the importance of the momentary conversation; in these she says that things pass and are lost that no book contains, and still the best that books have ever contained. Therefore she has made it my duty to preserve good individual thoughts which come from an intelligent conversation just as seeds come from a many-branched plant.

‡ to again confide in the guest that in that fashion an important archive had come into being, from which she many a time on sleepless nights read a page aloud to Makarie.

* . . . his friendly reception by the three who slowly appeared, finally turned into a conversation, where everyone contributed his part, the content of which however we condense briefly.

§ In the meantime we must not delay any longer and rather give the results at once than to obligate ourselves to have them appear bit by bit in the spirit of our readers. The following was yielded as the quintessence of what was discussed.

¶ This incident may after all have given rise to a conversation, traces of which we find in Ottilie's journal.

thought) or as "Keime von Gesprächen und Aufzeichnungen" (seeds of conversations and written accounts).[4]

Then there are other aphorisms that represent the condensed sense of a story, or if you will, the "moral" of a tale. Gidion refers to these as "Keimzellen von Geschichten" (seed cells of stories).[5] The most important example of this is to be found in that part of Wilhelm's prehistory which has here been called "Die Fischerknaben" (see above, pp. 68–75). It will be recalled that there Goethe used aphorism-like general statements as a sort of frame at the beginning, at the end, and in the middle of that narration. The most important of these was the one about the *Ruderpflock* (thole pin) which was related to the basic narrative by analogy. Others, however, are reflections on the general meaning of what has been reported. One of those from the center of the tale is as follows:

> Und wenn ich hier noch eine Betrachtung anknüpfe, so darf ich wohl bekennen: daß im Laufe des Lebens mir jenes erste Aufblühen der Außenwelt als die eigentliche Originalnatur vorkam, gegen die alles übrige, was uns nachher zu den Sinnen kommt, nur Kopien zu sein scheinen, die bei aller Annäherung an jenes doch des eigentlichen ursprünglichen Geistes und Sinnes ermangeln. (p. 274)*

There are other similar examples. The story of Wilhelm's medical studies is introduced thus:

> Die Unterhaltungen waren daher so belehrend als ergötzlich, denn die Freunde gaben sich wechselseitig Rechenschaft vom Gange des bisherigen Lebens und Tuns, woraus eine Bildung entstanden war, die sie wechselseitig erstaunen machte, dergestalt, daß sie sich untereinander erst selbst wieder mußten kennen lernen. (p. 322)†

Other examples would be found on pages 334 and 393.

One of the more important aspects of the *Fischerknaben* tale is the place in the novel that it occupies. Goethe sometimes uses juxtaposition to convey a hint, as he did by placing references to the *Kästchen*

---

* And if I here add an additional observation, so I may probably confess that in the course of life that first blooming of the external world seemed to me the real original nature, against which everything else that came to our senses later only seemed to be copies, which, however much they approached the former, still lacked the real original spirit and sense.

† The conversations were therefore as instructive as pleasant, for the friends gave each other a mutual account of the course up to then of their life and doings, from which an education arose which mutually astonished them so that they had to get acquainted once again.

in the Melusine tale (p. 376) just before Hersilie's letter to Wilhelm reporting that she now possesses both Felix's *Kästchen* and the key to it (pp. 376–78). Here, just after using the aphorisms as a frame for the *Fischerknaben* story, he ended Book II and inserted the first collection of maxims to appear, the "Betrachtungen im Sinne der Wanderer." And this with the foregoing is the justification mentioned earlier for considering the aphorisms as possible narrative insertions.

But it is not enough merely to recognize that a given aphorism is a kernel of a nonreported conversation or narrative; Goethe specifically challenges the reader to reverse the process and participate, if you will, in the further construction of the novel by inventing a conversation or a tale to fit a given maxim. He says of Wilhelm in Makarie's archive:

Hier nun mußte der Freund bescheiden zu Werke gehen, denn es fand sich nur allzuviel Anziehendes und Wünschenwertes; besonders achtete er die Hefte kurzer, kaum zusammenhängender Sätze höchst schätzenswert. Resultate waren es, die, wenn wir nicht ihre Veranlassung wissen, als paradox erscheinen, uns aber nötigen, vermittelst eines umgekehrten Findens und Erfindens rückwärtszugehen und uns die Filiation solcher Gedanken von weit her, von unten herauf wo möglich zu vergegenwärtigen. (pp. 124–25)‡

The above applies especially to using aphorisms as the basis for constructing imaginary conversations. Goethe hints that something similar should be done in using them as foundations for narratives, whether by analogy or not, not only in "Die Fischerknaben," but also in a reverse sort of way in "Die gefährliche Wette." There, it will be recalled, after having ended the tale, he invited the reader to construct a moral (p. 38).

Thus there are in the novel a large number of aphorisms (359 in the two collections alone) through which the reader is challenged to participate in structuring the work. Which are to be developed into

‡ Here now our friend had to go to work modestly because there was only too much that was attractive and desirable; he esteemed especially valuable the notebooks of short sentences which were hardly connected. They were results, which, if we do not know their cause, seem paradoxical, which require us however by means of a reversed finding and inventing to go backwards and to realize the derivation of such thoughts, from a distance, if possible from bottom upwards.

APHORISMS, MAXIMS AND REFLECTIONS

conversations, and which into narratives, is subjective. "Maximen und Reflexionen sind Ausdrucksformen, die auf der Grenze vom Dichterischen zum Denkerischen liegen, sie haben Teil an beiden Bereichen. . . . [Diese] Bundesgenossenschaft von Gedicht und Gehalt, von Schau und Sinn."*[6] Frequently the same aphorism could be dealt with in either way, and of course different readers will have different ideas. Sarter saw this aspect of Goethe's aesthetics: "Eine wichtige Forderung Goethescher Ästhetik ist: der erratenden, verbindenden, zurechtdenkenden Phantasie des Lesers soll im Kunstwerk weiter Spielraum gelassen werden." †[7] Stöcklein says: "Die grossen Aphorismenketten sind ungeschriebene Bücher" (the great chains of aphorisms are unwritten books).[8]

It is known that Goethe had long collected aphorisms. However, it would be an error to consider "Betrachtungen im Sinne der Wanderer" and "Aus Makariens Archiv" as random compilations from his files. A new aphorism was added to Makarie's archive according to an organization developed by the astronomer, who personally placed particularly difficult ones (p. 124), i.e., he fitted each into a related group of maxims.

Trunz (see n. 2 of this chapter) has proved that Goethe invested much time and effort in choosing which aphorisms from his collections to include in the novel, and in deciding on the order of their arrangement. Then, too, Flitner has demonstrated in detail just how he constructed "Aus Makariens Archiv" out of fourteen groups of interrelated aphorisms.[9] In other words, despite all appearances to the contrary, the two large collections of maxims and reflections constitute a carefully calculated part of the whole complex of the novel.

Goethe's distant and rather superior attitude to formal systems of philosophy is well known. He knew the classical philosophers, of course, and despite his personal acquaintance with the great figures of contemporary German idealistic philosophy, his distrust per-

---

* Maxims and reflections are forms of expression which lie on the border between the poetic and the philosophical; they participate in both realms. . . . [This] confederation of poem and content, of vision and meaning.

† It is an important demand of Goethe's aesthetics: wide room for action in the work of art is to be left to the guessing, connecting and adjusting imagination of the reader.

sisted. As he grew older, he came to look on aphorisms, and particularly groups of them, as his substitute, or answer, as it were, to philosophical systems.

Dabei kommt der Gruppe als einem Denk- und Verstehensorganismus besondere Bedeutung zu: Sie ist weder logisch, noch mechanisch, noch im zufälligen Sinne assoziativ, sie ist in keiner Weise herkömmlich systematisch oder gar schematisch komponiert; in ihr gestaltet sich vielmehr ein höchst empfindliches Pendeln zwischen isoliertem Satz und wechselseitigem Bezug—so erhält die Doppelbezeichnung "Maxime" und "Reflexion" im Sinne von "Resultat" und "Spiegelung" wichtige Bedeutung—zwischen grundsätzlicher Einsicht und modifizierendem Beispiel; die Aphorismengruppe wird zur unaufdringlichen Einübung in die morphologische Denkform, das vergleichende Verhalten zwischen Bild und Abgebildetem. . . . Die Gruppe ist nicht System, sondern lebendige "Gestalt"; in diesem gestalthaften Sinne vermag das scheinbar höchst Ordnungslose, der "Aphorismus," indem er sich zur Gruppe ordnet, dem Roman allererst "Einheit" zu geben.‡ [10]

Furthermore the aphorism, alone and in groups, is organic in the Goethean sense in that it reflects the unending natural process by which knowledge is advanced: one investigator forms his discoveries and the conclusions drawn therefrom into a challenge to the received body of knowledge in his specialty. In due course, then, another researcher, with differing facts and conclusions, in his turn challenges the accepted body of knowledge, including the ideas of his immediate predecessor. In discussing one of Goethe's aphorism series on scientific subjects,[11] Neumann says:

Nur durch Aphorismen läßt sich Erkenntnis als ein pulsierendes Wechselverhältnis von Einzelnem und Allgemeinem, von Anarchie und System, von Gehalt und Methode, Stoff und Form, "Lücke" und Zusammenhang, Wissenschaft und Kunst darstellen. Nur in ihnen läßt sich der Wider-

‡ In this connection special importance attaches to the group [of aphorisms] as an organism of thinking and understanding; it is neither logical nor mechanical, nor in the accidental sense associative; it is in no way traditionally systematically or even schematically constructed; in it there is formed, rather, a very sensitive alternation between an isolated sentence and a mutual relationship—so the double designation "maxim" and "reflection" in the sense of "result" or "mirroring" receives important meaning—between a basic insight and a modifying example; the aphorism group becomes an unobtrusive exercise in the morphological method of thinking, the comparative attitude between the picture and what is depicted. . . . The group is not a system, but rather a living "form"; in this formed sense that which is apparently highly lacking in order, the "aphorism," is capable, by being arranged in a group, of giving "unity" to the novel for the first time.

spruch, das Ineinanderwirken von Gegenkräften, die Vorstellung des Erkennens als eines "entdeckenden" Miteinander von Zettel und Einschlag in lebendiger Auseinandersetzung gestalten. . . . Der Aphorismus ist die einzige sprachliche Form, die die Darstellung der Erkenntnis *als* Konflikt "prägnant" ermöglicht. Hier tritt für Goethe der Begriff des "Symbolischen" ein.*

The aphorism possesses the further advantage from Goethe's point of view that it stimulates the reader to participate:

"Ordnungsformen" solcher Art sind Denkanstöße, die den Leser zur Komplettierung anreizen; nur so wird ein "System" möglich, das, als ein "individuelles Gesetz", flexibel genug bleibt, um die besondere Denkweise, das Denk"system" des verstehenden Individuums nicht zu zerstören. Nirgends ist die Aktivität des Lesers, seine Freiheit, innerhalb eines bestimmten Bezirks die "andere" Hälfte des Verstehensvorgangs zu ergänzen, so groß und sogleich von so großer Bedeutung wie im Aphorismus.†[12]

Neumann also recognizes that the aphorisms are in a sense "literary seeds."

Aphorismen als "literarische Sämereien" zu bezeichnen, is üblich. Die Aphorismusgruppen streuen Keime aus, die zu einer vielfältigen Saat aufgehen; ihre Ernte einzubringen, die Bezüge herzustellen, die den Roman zu einem Ganzen machen, ihn als die "Ernte" greifbar erscheinen lassen, die in den Keimen der Aphorismen angelegt war, gehört zum "Beschwerlichsten."‡[13]

Earlier in the chapter the double provenience of the aphorisms was

---

* Only by means of the aphorism can cognition be represented as a pulsating mutual relationship of the individual and the general, of anarchy and system, of content and method, material and form, "gap" and connection, science and art. Only in them can the contradiction be formed, the mutual interaction of opposing forces, the concept of cognition as a "discovering" unification of warp and woof in a living exposition. . . . The aphorism is the only form in language which makes possible in a "pregnant" way the presentation of cognition *as* conflict. Here, for Goethe, the concept of the "symbolic" sets in.

† Organizing forms of such a type are stimuli to thought which spur the reader on to complete them; only thus is a "system" possible, which, as an "individual law", remains flexible enough not to betray the special way of thinking, the thought "system" of the understanding individual. Nowhere [else] is the activity of the reader so great, his freedom within a definite area to fill out the "other" half of the process of understanding, and at the same time [nowhere else is the reader's activity] of so great importance as in the aphorism.

‡ It is usual to designate aphorisms as "literary seeds". The aphorism group sows seeds which grow into a manifold crop; to bring in the harvest, to produce the relationships which unify the novel, to make the novel comprehensible as the "harvest" which was sown in the seeds of the aphorisms, is the "most difficult" part.

noted; some appearing as kernels of conversations, some as seeds of a narrative. Many, possibly most, of the conversations dealt with questions of knowledge, as for instance that between Wilhelm and the astronomer on mathematics. So here is to be seen the juxtaposition and at the same time the tension between the scientific and the literary.

In the present study up to this point Goethe's process of organizing his literary work on principles gleaned from his scientific researches has been delineated: if for the moment it is pardonable to use a serious over-simplification for the sake of greater clarity, what has been described is how Goethe hung literary flesh on a scientific skelton. In connection with the aphorisms, however, this oversimplification is even less applicable than elsewhere, for here Goethe has brought the literary ("narrative") and scientific ("conversations") elements of his work into a new relationship. The groups and subgroups of aphorisms, some literary ("narrative"), some scientific ("conversations"), are of contrasting and yet complementary nature, so that in the resulting tension between them the work of art, the novel as a whole, gains a vital interest that is unique.

XV
THE GOETHEAN SERIES

IN HIS SCIENTIFIC STUDIES, Goethe had learned to look for and use a graduated series of phenomena. This is to be seen most easily, perhaps, in his essay on the intermaxillary bone, "Dem Menschen wie den Tieren ist ein Zwischenknocken der oberen Kinnlade zuzuschreiben (1784/1820)" ("An Intermediate Bone on the Upper Jaw Is to Be Ascribed to Man As Well As to the Animals").[1] For a long time it had been customary to claim that this bone was missing in man, which fact thus distinguished him from the beasts. In Goethe's discovery of the fallacy of this, his method of procedure is the important thing. One should, he said, "mehr ins Einzelne gehen und, bei genauer, stufenweiser Vergleichung mehrerer Tiere, vom Einfachsten bis auf das Zusammengesetztere, vom Kleinsten und Eingeengten auf das Ungeheuere und Ausgedehnte fortschreiten."*[2] As he developed his observations, it became clear that he used another type of series: he compared skulls of infants and the immature with those of adults, thus establishing a developmental series to be examined. Then he used still a third kind of series: he arranged various abnormalities in relation to the normal, and learned a great deal from malformations. Magnus says: "This method of serial arrangement of the phenomena to be investigated is really the one that Goethe made his very own. He employed it in nearly all his scientific studies, not only in the fields of botany and zoology, but also in mineralogy and optics. It brought him important results in plant and animal morphology."[3]

In his botanical studies he followed a similar course. For instance, he saw the leaves of the growing plant as a developmental series in his "Versuch, die Metamorphose der Pflanzen zu erklären" ("Attempt to

---

* go more into detail, and, with exact, step-by-step comparison of many animals, proceed from the simplest to the more complicated, from the smallest and most condensed to that which is huge and extended.

Explain the Metamorphosis of Plants," 1790).[4] In paragraphs 6, 7, and 8 of this essay he distinguished three kinds of metamorphosis, "die regelmäßige oder fortschreitende" (the regular or progressive), "die unregelmäßige oder rückschreitende" (the irregular or regressive) and "die zufällige" (the accidental) which was was caused by some accidental event. If one turns now to the families in the *Wanderjahre*, it is evident that the author considered the family of St. Joseph II as a regular or progressive metamorphosis, that he saw Odoard's domestic complications as an irregular or regressive metamorphosis, and since the mother is missing by the accident of death, the family of Wilhelm and Felix as an accidental metamorphosis. This habit of the poet's has been commented on elsewhere,[5] as well as his tendency to carry ways of thinking and observing that he had learned on his scientific pursuits over into his literary productions. An excellent example of this is his pervasive tendency to see the *Urform*, or archetype, and metamorphoses thereof, in all areas of life. As a matter of fact, the *Urform* with metamorphoses together make up, of course, a series, from the *Urform* as the most original to metamorphoses, each a little less original, genuine, or pure. And in his literary works, of course, the series does not have to be in the strict, logical, consecutive order that the scientific proof requires.

If this method of observation is applied to the *Wanderjahre* it is at once obvious that Goethe has here presented the reader with a large series (in the Goethean sense) of narrative insertions. They vary from the simplest, *Series 1*—an aphorism that is to be considered as the kernel of a narrative to be invented—through lengthier metamorphoses, to something as complex as Lenardo's three-part story.

Series 2. From another point of view (*wiederholte Spiegelungen*) one could consider the main plot as one narrative, to which others, the *Novellen*, are associated. Some are almost within the main plot, such as "St. Joseph II," others have a less direct connection, such as "Der Mann von funfzig Jahren," still others have almost no linkage, such as "Die pilgernde Törin."

Series 3. Wiederholte Spiegelungen, or the repeated mirrorings that have been mentioned several times and which other commentators have found in many parts of the novel, are in themselves a series of series.

Series 4 and 5. But the narratives break down into series in yet another fashion. Near the beginning there are three novellas that

THE GOETHEAN SERIES

form a group, "St. Joseph II," "Die pilgernde Törin," and "Wer ist der Verräter?" Near the end is another group of three, "Die neue Melusine," "Die gefährliche Wette," and "Nicht zu weit." It will be noted that the first group contains largely positive examples and the second group largely negative ones, although each group has an exception. In the first, as the *Törin's* story ends, her fate has not yet been finally decided; she is, so to speak, in a state of suspended animation. Her untrue fiancé *could* still appear and resolve everything happily, but it looks quite unlikely. In the last group "Die neue Melusine" forms an exception in that there things almost worked out well. In each series the exception "points to" the other series, thus:

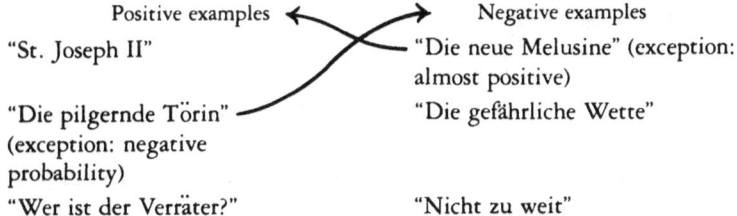

Positive examples   Negative examples
"St. Joseph II"   "Die neue Melusine" (exception: almost positive)
"Die pilgernde Törin" (exception: negative probability)   "Die gefährliche Wette"
"Wer ist der Verräter?"   "Nicht zu weit"

Series 6 and 7. Above the narrative insertions with and without love affairs were compared, and here too the exceptions "point to" the other group (see p. 82).

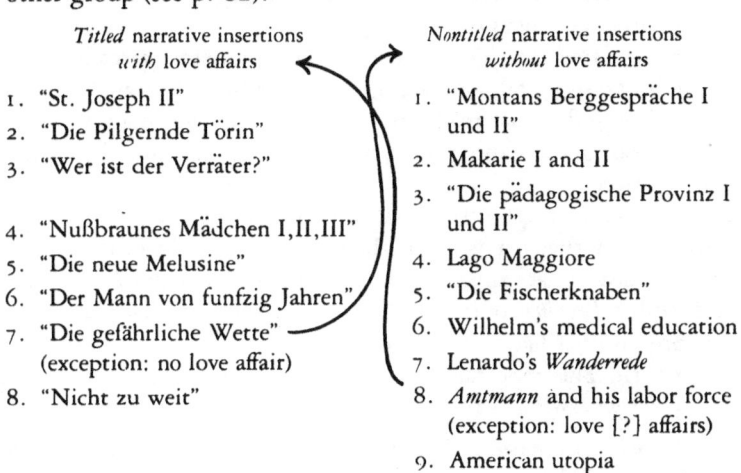

Titled narrative insertions *with* love affairs
1. "St. Joseph II"
2. "Die Pilgernde Törin"
3. "Wer ist der Verräter?"
4. "Nußbraunes Mädchen I, II, III"
5. "Die neue Melusine"
6. "Der Mann von funfzig Jahren"
7. "Die gefährliche Wette" (exception: no love affair)
8. "Nicht zu weit"

Nontitled narrative insertions *without* love affairs
1. "Montans Berggespräche I und II"
2. Makarie I and II
3. "Die pädagogische Provinz I und II"
4. Lago Maggiore
5. "Die Fischerknaben"
6. Wilhelm's medical education
7. Lenardo's *Wanderrede*
8. *Amtmann* and his labor force (exception: love [?] affairs)
9. American utopia

Here it is graphically apparent just what Goethe meant when he had the baroness in the "Unterhaltungen deutscher Ausgewanderten" (conversations of German emigrants) say: "Ich liebe mir sehr Parallelgeschichten, *eine deutet auf die andere hin* und erklärt ihren Sinn besser als viele trockene Worte" (WA I 18.190, italics added).†

Series 8. In addition, of course, the above constitutes in a fashion a double series; there are here at the same time series of titled and nontitled insertions, and ones with and without love affairs.

Series 9. There is another obvious series here; Goethe shows a marked predeliction to telling the parts of his story in two increments, or what might be called a series of pairs.

		I		II
1.	Montan's *Berggespräche*	p. 30		p. 259
2.	*Die pädagogische Provinz*	149		244
3.	*Lenardos Tagebuch*	338		414
4.	*Amerikapläne*	332		405
5.	Wilhelm's prehistory	"Fischerknaben" 268	Medical ed.	332
6.	Makarie	114		436
7.	Aphorisms	"Betrachtungen," 283	"Makariens"	460
8.	Recruiting speeches	Lenardo's 383	Odoard's	408

Series 10. Another important series is the one previously dealt with, namely, the novellas that detail the past history of each of the more important members of the emigrant league. That comprised seven narrative insertions.

Series 11 and 12. The collections of aphorisms, already noted above in the series of pairs, are used also for two additional types of series. The individual reader is left to use his own imagination in turning part of them into illustrative narratives, part into illustrative conversations.

Series 13. The aphorisms that are outside the collections would form still another list, such as the ones on the walls of the uncle's castle, those that appeared in Montan's *Berggespräche*, in the *pädagogische Provinz*, or the ones left by Wilhelm on "das Blatt" with Susanne and her fiancé (p. 426).

Series 14. The important conversations that take place throughout the novel would form the next group. It is difficult to make a list

† I love parallel stories; one indicates another and explains its meaning better than many dry words.

here, as they would range from Felix's childish questioning of his father at the beginning through the *Berggespräche* with Montan, the pedagogical province to Lenardo's *Wanderrede* and the American plans.

Series 15. Blood-related families: from the point of view of families, the start to a series could be the key symbolism mentioned in the next chapter, which stands for the mutual male-female attraction. Or one could consider the Wilhelm-Felix family as the smallest (disregarding the previous possibility as being only potential), and construct a series to the large blood families, such as that of the uncle, Makarie, Hersilie, Juliette, and Lenardo, with their American connections; the negative example, or the regressive metamorphosis, would be "Nicht zu weit."

Series 16. It is also possible to consider an association of people without blood relationship as a "family." A series might begin here with the smallest group, say the *Sammler* (collector) and his assistant, proceed to a larger one, say the four at the Lago Maggiore, then to the students and their instructors at "Die pädagogische Provinz," then to the league of emigrants, or to the mountain weavers, with a negative example (regressive metamorphosis) being "Die gefährliche Wette."

Series 17. There are a number of accidental metamorphoses of the family, beginning with Wilhelm and Felix, then the Major and Flavio, the Major's sister and Hilarie, the uncle plus nieces Hersilie and Juliette, and nephew Lenardo, the Revannes senior and junior.

Series 18. There are men unsatisfactory for forming a family in "Die pilgernde Törin" and "Die neue Melusine." Note that there is only one instance of a woman unfitted for family life, Albertina in the last tale!

Series 19. Love affairs across the generations: Wilhelm and Hersilie and the Major and Hilarie.

Series 20. There is a series of what are here called "triangle pictures." The triangle of misery that ends "Nicht zu weit" is most effective (p. 404). There are others, not all tragic, where three people join in a momentary picture that shows the essence of their relationship. In "Der Mann von funfzig Jahren," Flavio and Hilarie are interrupted by the Major while skating in the moonlight (p. 214); in "Wer ist der Verräter?" Lucidor before the mirror *thinks* he sees his beloved Lucinde kissing the Italian visitor Antoni (p. 99); and most effective is the triangle of Lenardo, *der Gehilfe*, and Susanne by the bedside of her dying father (p. 434).

Series 21. In several places the reader hears of a series of paintings that have pedagogical value, for instance, the uncle's collection of portraits (p. 79), Makarie's gallery (p. 115), the Old and New Testament galleries in the pedagogical province (pp. 149–61), and portraits of important political leaders collected by the old family friend in "Wer ist der Verräter?" (p. 102).

Series 22. The education of the heroes is a matter of continuing concern: Lucidor in *Verräter*, Felix in the *Provinz*, Wilhelm in Wilhelm's medical education (pp. 323f), while Odoard's military academy (p. 396) is a regressive metamorphosis.

Series 23, 24, and 25, all within "Wer ist der Verräter?" Lucidor has a series of monologues, a series of attempted flights, and four scenes before the "magic" mirror.

Series 26. Makarie helps a number of people in different ways: the uncle (by hearing his weekly confession, p. 84), Wilhelm (p. 119), Lenardo (p. 128), "die schöne Witwe" from "Der Mann von funfzig Jahren" (p. 224), Susanne and the mountain weaver folk (pp. 446f), and the girls in Makarie's girls' school (p. 123).

Series 27. One might speak of a chirurgical series: Wilhelm's showing of the *Besteck* to Montan, "Die Fischerknaben," Wilhelm's medical education, and the last scene in the novel, when he restores his own son Felix to life.

Series 28. There is of course a Lenardo series also, as pointed out above (pp. 39–51).

Series 29. A recurring problem in the various love affairs mentioned is the question of the property or the position that the new couple will have. This was noted in "Wer ist der Verräter?," it makes an important element in "Der Mann von funfzig Jahren," and is significant for Odoard in "Nicht zu weit."

Series 30. And finally, since Goethe began his comparative study of animal skulls (in his search for the intermaxillary bone in man) with that of the "unimportant" mouse (the other end of the list being the skull of the elephant), one should end this list of series, or perhaps should have begun it, with another small, "unimportant" feature: the heroes of two of the negative tales, "Die neue Melusine" (p. 375) and "Die gefährliche Wette" (p. 380) are left-handed!

The above listing of the various series in the novel makes no pretension to being exhaustive; it is meant instead to be suggestive. However, a few things are indisputably clear. First, the novel is a large series of series; exactly how many is uncertain, but the number is considerable. Secondly, the principle of the series as Goethe understood it is one of the most important single elements of form operating in this work of art. These series bind the main plot together, and they tie the parts to the whole. And, not least important, since any given feature of the novel may appear in two or more series, the series are interwoven with each other, and so serve in this fashion also to bind the whole together into an artistic unity.

Goethe wrote Zauper in 1821 about the novel: ". . . ist es nicht aus einem Stück, so ist es doch aus einem Sinn."‡[6] If one applies to the novel the methods of procedure that Goethe learned from his long and intense devotion to science, namely the concept of *Urform* and metamorphosis (with the three kinds of metamorphosis), the family as *Urform* and metamorphosis, and the Goethean series, then it is undeniable that there is far more artistic unity and cohesion here than the unsuspecting reader can possibly see at first acquaintance. As Goethe said about his own *Wahlverwandtschaften*: "Das Buch muß . . . d r e i m a l gelesen werden."*[7]

---

‡ . . . if it isn't all of one piece, it is all of one meaning.
* The book has to be read *three times*.

XVI
THE *WANDERJAHRE* AS *SCHLÜSSELROMAN*

UNFORTUNATELY ENGLISH does not have a word to describe the novel form known on the continent either as a *roman à clef* or as a *Schlüsselroman*. Since the present discussion concerns a work of Goethe's, the German term will be used.

Actually the term refers to two somewhat different things: the older and apparently original usage was to designate a tale in which some or all of the characters and places were given code names for actual people or localities. Examples would be Sannazaro's *Arcadia* (1495), *Theuerdank* by Emperor Maximilian with Melchior Pfinzing (1517), Margaret of Navarre's *Heptaméron des nouvelles* (1559), d'Urfey's *Astrée*, or several of Mme de Scudéri's novels. Goethe was familiar with many of these. Friends of the author, or other insiders who knew the "key" to the novel, would then know that Theuerdank was really Emperor Maximilian I, and so forth. Sometimes the key would be published and either distributed separately or else bound as a preface or appendix to the work.

This had become somewhat old-fashioned by the time that Goethe began to write: the more usual meaning of *Schlüsselroman* in his day was a work in which the author described his own experiences with pseudonyms for the persons and/or places concerned. So when *Werther* appeared readers long annoyed Goethe by trying to find out the disguised, or "verschlüsselte," elements in the author's experience which lay behind the events of the novel.[1]

The word *Schlüsselroman* does not occur in the novel, which is hardly surprising. Nor is it unusual that a key plays a role of some importance in reference to the little box or *Kästchen* which is clearly a central symbol in the work. What is highly unusual is that Goethe provides the reader with a drawing or sketch of that particular key

(p. 321). Questions immediately arise: a case of surgical instruments (*Besteck*) plays a central role in Wilhelm's professional life, yet there is no drawing of it; nor is there one of the important thole-pin (*Ruderpflock*). Paintings play a vital role in the story of St. Joseph II, which opens the novel, and although that tale is in a sense a model for the remainder of the *Wanderjahre*, still no sketches are included. The scene in front of the *Ahnentafel* (family tree) is central to "Der Mann von funfzig Jahren," yet the reader is left to imagine what that painted family tree looked like. Instances could be added, but the question remains, why did Goethe find it desirable to include a drawing of this particular object? He did not do so on a transitory whim. The drawing first appeared in the version of 1821, and when the author prepared the extensively rewritten and expanded final version in 1829 for the *Ausgabe letzter Hand*, he had the sketch reprinted, merely changing it from the horizontal to the vertical position.

The case is also quite rare in European literature; one searches memory in vain for a comparable instance. Illustrated novels are not unheard of, but usually the illustrations are provided by a special artist for a later edition of a novel that has become popular. Some humorous novels, such as Swift's *Gulliver's Travels* or Sterne's *Tristram Shandy*, contain graphic jokes, but in this serious novel the poet himself provided the sketch as a part of the original work. And is this merely an illustration? If it is more than that—a symbol, say—why, of the many symbols in the work, was this one alone picked out for special treatment? It is submitted that this is "ein offenbares Geheimnis" (an open secret) such as Goethe loved, a puzzle with which he is wordlessly challenging the reader. If such be the case, then the *Wanderjahre* may indeed be looked on as a *Schlüsselroman*, but in a completely new and individual sense. Goethe would then be following his lifelong habit: when he borrowed from mythical or literary tradition, he transformed things, sometimes radically, to suit his own purposes. To cite a few instances: the plot and character of his *Iphigenia* differ significantly from the classical drama of Euripides; in the Greek myth of Ganymede, Zeus kidnaps and carries off to heaven the handsome youth, whereas Goethe depicts the young man as rising spontaneously to Olympus out of his intense longing to be united with the divine; the seemingly traditional and churchly elements in the last scenes of *Faust II* differ sharply in their underlying philosophy from traditional theology.

In this study we have been repeatedly observing Goethe's use of the family, both as archetype (*Urform*) and metamorphosis thereof, as the backbone and central thread of the literary work. The family of St. Joseph II is a model and an ideal of this archetype of human association. The Wilhelm-Felix family, lacking as it does a mother, is a metamorphosis ("accidental") of the *Urform*, as are the Revannes, father and son, the family of the *Oheim*, etc. In the various love affairs, single individuals are observed attempting to unite with their beloveds to form their own new family nucleus—Felix and Hersilie, Wilhelm and Natalie, Lucidor and Lucinde, and others. As has been shown, Goethe learned in his anatomical and osteological studies to arrange related phenomena in a carefully graded series, which he would then study intently. As we have been seeing, he has been doing something comparable with the family, as *Urform* and as *Metamorphose* in the *Wanderjahre*, except that since the latter is a work of art rather than science, the family series does not need to be arranged in a careful step-by-step order. To return to the key: does this enigmatic drawing then play any role in one of the series under observation in the novel so far? Before attempting an answer, it is necessary to examine the text more closely.

As is so often the case, Goethe scatters his comments on the key throughout a wide section of the novel—chapters 2, 7, and 17 of Book III—relying apparently on the imprecise memory of the superficial reader to fail to grasp all of the meaning which might have been too clear if all the material were to appear consecutively. Here, then, is another aspect of Goethe's "offenbares Geheimnis," his method of hiding things, paradoxical as that may sound, right out in the open. The first reference to the key (pp. 320–21) is in a letter from Hersilie to Wilhelm. She has found the key in a jacket that had belonged to the urchin Fitz. Goethe probably knew that the name *Fitz* was used in England in post-Norman times to designate someone's illegitimate son; Fitzwilliam being the natural son of William, for example. The fact that the key turned up in the pocket of this *Gassenjunge*, a thief, a rascal, an associate of smugglers, among other things, is enough to raise an eyebrow. But then when Hersilie is moved to keep her find a secret and at the same time think of

Wilhelm with some excitement, even though she knows she is doing wrong, despite her pangs of conscience—all of this leads one to hear suggestively erotic overtones. It is notable that she does not turn at this juncture, say, to her uncle or to her aunt Makarie. She wants Wilhelm present and thinks ceaselessly of him with strongly beating heart, in which connection she thinks of the seventh commandment! The erotic element is thus finally strongly and explicitly present. She then closes her letter with a postscript which seems to reverse much of what she has just said by recalling that the *Kästchen* (the box whose lock the key fits) really belongs to Felix, and that he too should thus be called. It should be noted in passing that the key Faust used in Part II has been seen in various interpreters (including C. G. Jung) as a phallic symbol.

The next reference to the key occurs in the seventh chapter (pp. 377–78). The older collector who had originally taken the *Kästchen* on deposit has died, and his successor now appears at the uncle's estate, wishing to deposit the same with the uncle's court. The latter, knowing Hersilie's interest in Wilhelm, gave it to her. She again reported by letter to Wilhelm: ". . . genug, hier liegt das Kästchen vor mir in meiner Schatulle, der Schlüssel daneben, und wenn Sie eine Art von Herz und Gemüt haben, so denken Sie, wie mir zu Mute ist, wieviele Leidenschaften sich in mir herumkämpfen, wie ich Sie herwünsche, auch wohl Felix dazu" (p. 378).* Here too the erotic note is as clear as possible.

The final reference to the key occurs in the scene in which Felix stormily declares his love for Hersilie and tries to open the casket, only to have the key break off in the lock (pp. 457–58). He then kisses Hersilie forcefully; she returns the kiss despite herself, before she angrily orders him away. Sexual elements are unmistakably predominant here also. Later Hersilie reported that the key had not been broken, but that it turns out to have consisted of two parts held together by a magnetic attraction, which parts then separated under Felix's passionate and violent manipulation. At this point the reader would like to look again at the key diagram, but Goethe has "incon-

* . . . enough, here is the little box lying before me in my jewel case, the key beside it, and if you have any kind of heart and feeling, think how I feel, how many passions are struggling within me, how [much] I wish you were here, also probably Felix too.

veniently" placed it with the first reference to the key, 15 chapters and 130-odd pages earlier. The location of the magnetic joint in the key is of course not indicated, but most likely it was at the juncture of the handle and the shaft. The illustration shows a reproduction of the key as it appears in the text, with a dashed line to indicate the handle-shaft joint.

Before going further it should be recalled that the key does not always work; sometimes it opens the *Kästchen*, sometimes it does not. The old goldsmith and jeweler friend of Hersilie's uncle, the same who discovered the magnetic joint, was able to open the box from a distance *without* use of the key (p. 458), while Felix had been unable to open it *with* the key. Hersilie reports to Wilhelm: ". . . sie [die Teile des Schlüssels] sind magnetisch verbunden, halten einander fest, aber schließen nur dem Eingeweiten" (p. 458).† Later she refers to "den Schlüssel, der nicht schließt."‡

There has been a good deal of speculation about the meaning of the little box or *Kästchen* and only a little less about the key.[2] As far as the *Kästchen* is concerned, the present intention is to follow rather closely the suggestions made by Emrich in his 1952 article. He starts out by recognizing the multiple levels of symbolic meaning in the novel and the mutual mirroring of the various parts. He then sums up the most likely meanings, warning however that no one meaning is to be predominant, but that all are important, and that there are more in addition, and, to be sure, all meanings are present at the same time.

1. The *Kästchen* represents the secret of (geologic) nature. Both granite, which for Goethe symbolized forces of conservation, and basalt, which for him represented revolutionary forces, are present.[3]

---

† . . . they [the parts of the key] are joined magnetically, held firmly to one another, but function only for the initiated.
‡ the key that does not operate [or function].

2. The box also stands for gold in the sense that Goethe used it in *Faust II*, symbol of the highest poetic power of the mind and at the same time symbol of destructive forces.

3. It is a symbol referring to the Old Testament tree of knowledge—man becomes guilty, sinful.

4. It is a sexual symbol—womb (*Kästchen*) and phallus (key).

5. The key. He cites Goethe's description, "Pfeile mit Widerhaken" (arrows with barbs). But, he says, this is hardly Cupid's arrow. Instead he notes how the lower part, the *Widerhaken* (barb) resembles the Greek letter *chi* (which traditionally stands for Christ, of course), and notes further: ". . . der obere [Teil] geht wahrscheinlich auf Freimaurersymbole zurück (Emrich, p. 348).* Two pages later he says: "Er ist in der Tat der Schlüssel zu dem Gesamtwerk" (it is in fact the key to the whole work) in the sense that it conceals yet reveals.

6. *Kästchen* and key, Emrich suggests, are also "Sinnbilder für die Integration der menschlichen Persönlichkeit in Gemeinschaft, Religion, fur eine Vereinigung aller getrennten Sphären in der Seele, im sozialen Leben, in der Geschichte der Völker und Religionen."† Then he summarizes:

Das Kästchen- und Schlüsselsymbol macht uns aber in einem wunderbar eindringlichen Bild das "offenbare Geheimnis" der Poesie selbst anschaulich. Offenbaren, öffnen, und zugleich verhüllen, verschließen, beides wird im Schlüssel und Kästchen versinnbildlicht. In diesem Sinne sind beide gleichsam Symbol des Symbolischen selbst, komprimiertestes Sinnbild aller poetischen Sinnbilder.‡

To this must be added another element that Emrich does not mention, something like the achievement of an ideal family life. If Hersilie and Felix had been able to open the *Kästchen*, the act would have symbolized the final, happy resolution of their love. The fact

---

* . . . the upper [part] apparently goes back to masonic symbols.

† symbols for the integration of human personality into community, religion, for a uniting of separated spheres in the soul, in social life, in the history of nations and religions.

‡ The casket-and-key symbol makes apparent to us in one wonderfully impressive picture the "open secret" of poetry itself. To reveal, to open, and at the same time to conceal, to lock up, both are symbolized in key and casket. In this sense both are, so to speak, symbol of the symbolic itself, the most compressed symbol of all poetic symbols.

that they could not can be interpreted as due perhaps in part to Hersilie's contrariness in alternately attracting and repelling Felix, and to his headlong, passionate, and violent attempt to discover the secret of the *Kästchen*, which causes him to "break" the key in two.

So far attention has been directed primarily at the *Kästchen*; it is now time to return specifically to the key. In general terms, Cirlot's *Dictionary of Symbols* draws attention to the similarity of the key and the Egyptian anserated cross, the *Nem Ankh*, the symbol of life. Bachofen notes that in antiquity the key was related symbolically to the underworld, and symbolized the opening of the womb of earth for plant growth (in spring), and thus also in human terms, birth.[4] Friedrich Ohly has proposed some very interesting ideas about the key.[5] He notes that Goethe had been reading Kästner's novel *Die Agape oder die geheime Weltbund der Christen* (*Agape Or the Secret World League of Christians*), published in Jena in 1819. He discussed the novel with friends, and noted in his diary for 23 July 1819: "Kästners *Agape* und Schlüssel dazu. Zeichnung des alten Turms und Umgebung" ("Kästner's *Agape* and key to it. Drawing of the old tower and surroundings"). Ohly goes on to note that the diary then records work on the *Wanderjahre*. Plate I of his article is reproduced below, from which it is clear that the two hieroglyphics from Kästner's novel do indeed have a resemblance to the key of the *Wander-*

3) Zu ihren Insignien gehörte wahrscheinlich ⚵ ,
welches Zeichen auch das Fundament ihres Geheim
alphabets gewesen zu seyn scheint. [79])

Fünfte Stufe oder Rittergrad.

Ihre Loosung war: Ich habe Muth und Schwerdt. [80])

Ein Schwerdt mag daher auch zu ihren Insignien gehört haben.

Eins ihrer Kennzeichen war vermuthlich: ☧
(Jesus Christus Rex, Jesus Christus König.) [81])

jahre. What he fails to appreciate adequately is that the Kästner symbols are apparently totally religious and Christian. Ohly attempts to relate them to the *pädagogische Provinz* and the three *Ehrfurchten* (three reverences), overlooking the fact, first, that in the *Wanderjahre* there is no connection between the pedagogical province and the casket-key symbolism, and second, that the casket-key symbolism in its every appearance contains strong erotic overtones, which are apparently completely lacking in the Kästner novel.[6] Consequently, interesting as the similarities Ohly has discovered are, they should probably be discounted as largely coincidental.

A close look at the diagrammed key is now in order. Despite Hersilie's works, "Erinnert es nicht an Pfeile mit Widerhaken?" ("Doesn't it remind you of arrows with barbs?" p. 321), it does *not* look particularly like arrows with barbs. We shall return later to a consideration of the reasons why Goethe should have implied that it did. In the key, the elements that cross the shaft at the bottom seem to suggest two circles, one on each side of the shaft. If one imagines the shaft and the circles without, for the moment, the upper quadrangle, the suggestion of a phallus is quite clear. And this in turn recalls some pornographic doodling that Goethe did on one occasion, doodling that has survived (see illustration).[7]

These sketches in turn are clearly linked to an explanation Goethe

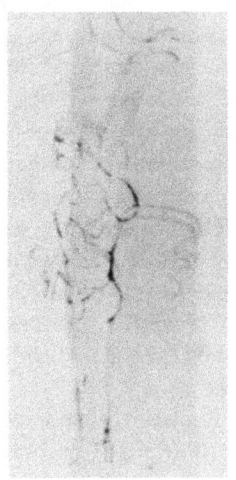
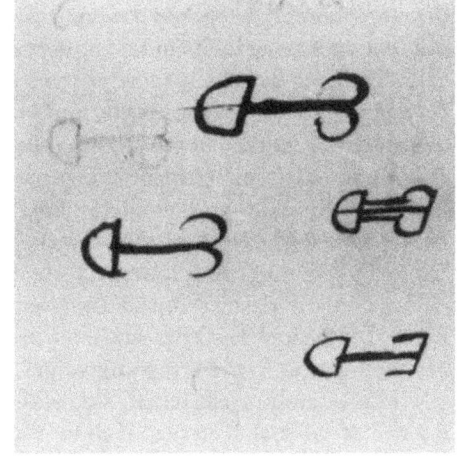

wrote about 1790 for his Duke Karl August of the renaissance text *Priapeia*, which, in Latin, discussed sexual customs of antiquity. Carmen LIV of this collection reads as follows: [8]

> E D si scribas, temonemque insuper addas,
> Qui medium D vult scindere, pictus erit.

(If you write E D, and add a dash in between,
Which cuts the middle of the D, it will be depicted.)

To this Goethe added for Karl August (in Latin!):

This verse teaches us that we ought to place this before our eyes. To be understood thus. If you write E D and add a dash, indeed the thicker line thus directed should divide the D in the middle and a phallus will be drawn. Indeed children and rather uncultured men are accustomed to produce pictures like this. The reason for this is that we see in the dash the neck of the phallus represented, in the same way children are accustomed to represent the arms and legs of men. [9]

The drawing reproduced above is apparently Goethe's effort to "place this before our eyes." Noteworthy here is how the curved strokes of the manuscript capital E suggest two circles, as do the cross members of the key. In other words, the lower portion of the depicted key bears a close resemblance to the E plus dash, to erotic symbols Goethe was familiar with and used. Furthermore, as we have seen, the erotic notes have been strong on every occasion on which the key has been mentioned. There is visible here furthermore the first steps in the process by which Goethe transformed a simple descriptive sketch, the phallus on the Herm, into a symbol, the lower half of the key. In the E D sketches reproduced by Femmel, Goethe, moving from right to left, experimented first with a squared E and then with a rounded E, and then sketched in the completion of the suggested circles. The dash is indicated once lightly, then heavily, then with a triple line. In the sketch from *Priapeia* the movement is from left to right, and the dash is unusually elongated. Finally in the lower portion of the key the D has vanished, replaced by the square handle, yet the relation to the foregoing stages is clear.

Unfortunately on the female side of the key symbol we do not have a series of Goethe sketches to show the evolution of the oval *cista mystica* into the square with rings, but it is not really necessary. It can

THE *WANDERJAHRE* AS *SCHLÜSSELROMAN*

be assumed that a stylization process took place comparable to the one observed in the male half of the symbol.

The upper half of the key, the handle, does not, however, resemble a D and thus remains to be dealt with. Here Emrich and Ohly believe they see reflections of symbols taken from Freemasonry.[10] But if this be the case, what is the connection between Freemasonry and the key-*Kästchen* symbolism as Goethe used it in the *Wanderjahre*? However, Ohly has pointed in the right direction in another article.[11] Here he examines in some detail the Greek κίστη which was a central feature in the Eleusinian mysteries, and the Roman *cista mystica*, which latter was much reproduced in Roman grave monuments, and which Goethe had surely noted during his Italian stay. As a matter of fact, he later (c. 1810) drew a sketch of the Roman *cista*, apparently while copying a coin (see illustration).[12]

Ohly cites a number of classical authorities, from a perusal of whose works the following picture emerges.[13] In the fifth and fourth centuries B.C. the κίστη of the Eleusinian mysteries (secret, of course) was a container of basketry, usually round or oval, with a lid. It was of moderate size, and had numerous rings around the sides and on the top through which thongs or ribbons were passed to carry the ceremonial basket in formal processions. The basket contained a reproduction of the female genitalia of the goddess Demeter. The idea was that the neophyte should, in a secret ceremony, take the reproduction from the box, and pass it over his body to symbolize his emergence from the goddess's womb in a second birth as her devotee, or disciple, or child. By the way, somewhat similar ceremonies were carried out in antiquity to symbolize the adoption of a child.

By late Roman times, the *cista* was no longer necessarily associated with the cult of Demeter and was made of various materials; some that were made of bronze have survived. Opposite is a reproduction of a square bronze *cista mystica* such as Goethe might have seen in fact or on a grave relief: note the rings at the sides and on top to take the carrying straps or thongs. What the poet has apparently done in the key drawing is to stylize the affair in a view from above, with circles at the corners and in the center to represent the original carrying rings. During this later Roman period the *cistae* often contained feminine cosmetic items and were little more than an equivalent of the modern lady's purse. It is important to note, however, that Goethe knew of the Greek symbolism. In the twelfth Roman Elegy he specifically mentions Demeter and Eleusis, as he and his beloved, imagining they have been returned to ancient times, watch a repetition of the Eleusinian procession.

The elegy makes it quite clear that the poet associated erotic feelings with the Eleusinian festival. As the poet, he observes to his beloved: "Sind zwei Liebende doch sich ein versammeltes Volk" (Two lovers are for each other, after all, a collected people). Here, then, the pair are not just a couple, but think of themselves as parents of a whole people as their progeny multiply. The poem goes on to mention the κίστη, which Goethe here calls a *Kästchen*, and then he continues:

> Und was war das Geheimnis, als daß Demeter, die große,
>   Sich gefällig einmal auch einem Helden bequemt,
> Als sie Jasion einst, dem rüstigen König der Kreter,
>   *Ihres unsterblichen Leibes holdes Verborgene gegönnt.*
>   (Ll. 23–26, italics added)*

The poet then ends with the following to his lady-love:

>   Verstehst du nun, Geliebte, den Wink?
>   Jene buschige Myrte beschattet ein heiliges Plätzchen!
> Unsere Zufriedenheit bringt keine Gefährde der Welt. (Ll. 32–34)†

---

   * And what was the secret, except that Demeter, the great one,
     Had once acquiesced agreeably to a hero
   When she long ago granted to Jasion, active king of the Cretans,
     The dear hidden places of her immortal body.
   †   Do you now understand, beloved, the gesture?
   That bushy myrtle over there shades a holy spot,
     And our satisfaction will bring no danger to the world.

Art of the Etruscans (126 photos by Walter Dräyer; Martin Hurlimann. Text: Massimo Pallotino, London, 1955)

Thus Goethe's understanding of the Eleusinian κίστη is clear: for him it symbolized that which it had contained in reproduction in Greek times, the female genitalia.

To return to the key: the upper, rectangular portion can easily be understood as a stylized κίστη, with loops or rings at the corners and in the center for the carrying thongs. Goethe's only departure from the Greek original is that he makes it rectangular, as the Romans did, rather than round or oval. Thus one sees the key to consist of male and female symbols, each so sharply stylized as to be for all intents and purposes disguised. And at this point it is possible to understand a little better Hersilie's remark that the key looked like arrows with barbs. The sleight-of-hand artist, in practising his ancient craft, misdirects the attention of his audience to something inconsequential while he carries out his secret manipulation, secure in the knowledge that people will see, not what is in front of their eyes, but what they are told that they will see. Goethe has simply borrowed a bit of the technique of these timeless mountebanks—by telling his readers that the key looks like arrows with barbs he has guaranteed that everyone will dutifully look for, and of course find, that resemblance. If he had omitted such a misleading hint, it is much more likely that many would have hit on the actual symbolic content.

The key, then, in its male and female components, joined as they are by a "magnetic" attraction, represents human sexuality. But by what right does one reach such a conclusion, after having discarded the religious and masonic symbolism that Emrich and Ohly believed they had found in the same key? First of all, the hypothesis here advanced explains the strong sexual and erotic overtones noted in every reference in the text to the key, as the other does not. Even more important, it is an element (a key element if you will) in the Goethean series of the family as an archetype and its metamorphosis that has been observed throughout this work of art. How can one reduce the human family to its simplest and most original terms? Male and female, if united sexually, will produce offspring, from which moment on a family is in existence. And so the key symbolism is, in both the temporal and organic senses, the simplest and original archetype of the family. Thus Goethe was justified in departing from tradition so far as to include a drawing of the key in his novel. In a sense undreamed of by his contemporaries, the *Wanderjahre* is in fact a *Schlüsselroman*.

It will be recalled that the chest could be opened without use of the key, for the old goldsmith had done so (p. 458), but then he was old, wise, and "initiated" (*eingeweiht*). The fact that there is not only a key but also a keyhole and a lock for it to engage indicate that the usual, normal path to the values and valuables locked inside the chest is through human sexuality. But neither half of the key, neither male nor female sexuality alone will suffice.

It should be noted that it is sexuality, properly understood, that is needed. Hersilie erred in her indecision between Wilhelm and Felix, in her coquettishness in alternately attracting and repelling Felix. Felix made the mistake of impetuously crushing Hersilie to him and forcing his kisses on her. When he then used this same excessive force trying to open the little chest, the key "broke" in two.

Human sexuality, properly used and understood, results in a family, and thus makes accessible the treasures locked in the little casket. This is the sense of the tale about "Saint" Joseph and his Maria, this is what Lucidor and Lucinde learned, this is apparently what will be denied to the *pilgernde Törin*. The needed male-female harmony could be achieved by Melusine's lover only for a short time. The Major and the beautiful widow, Flavio and Hilarie, learn to be successful, while Odoard and Albertina never come close. Lenardo and his *nußbraunes Mädchen* learn slowly how to achieve the proper relationship. The reader is left to assume that Wilhelm and his Natalie have already learned it and are now looking forward to consummation of their desires.

Before leaving the key a comment on Goethe's sense of humor is in order. As is well known, he was severely criticized by his more puritanical contemporaries for being immoral, not only in his personal life (for instance his long-standing relationship with Christine Vulpius) but also in his works. His old friend Herder had called the *Lehrjahre* "dein Bordellroman" (your bordello novel), and in his *Wahlverwandtschaften* the central scene of the double vicarious adultery had outraged many. In his old age the wise old gentleman of Weimar was reputed to be Jovian in his superiority and reserve. And yet, when he contemplated, as he must have, the reaction that some of his contemporaries would have had for the key symbolism, if they had only known what it was, one can only believe that the dignified *Herr Geheimrath* allowed himself at least a concealed Olympian smile.

XVII
CONCLUSION

WHEN GOETHE modifies a model, there are four elements in the process which, if taken together, give an unmistakable insight into his ultimate artistic purposes: first, what parts of the model he adopted; secondly, what parts he adopted with changes; thirdly, what parts he discarded; and finally, where and what new parts of his own he added. As was noted above in the discussion of "St. Joseph II" these criteria show to what a great extent the first narrative insertion is a model for the novel to follow, despite the fact that the tale is not really a novella, despite the fact that its hero is not really a saint. Here the reader sees the extraordinary extent to which the family, conceived as the *Urzelle* (primal cell) of human association, forms the red thread, so to speak, that runs through the entire work, from "St." Joseph clear to the symbolism of the key.

Intimately joined to the family is the *Urphänomen* (archetype) and its metamorphosis. If the family as *Urform* is to be found in "St. Joseph II," there are a large number of metamorphoses of it in the remainder of the novel, such as the progressive or normal metamorphosis in "Wer ist der Verräter?," the regressive or abnormal metamorphosis of it in "Die neue Melusine," and an accidental metamorphosis in Wilhelm and Felix.

Furthermore the principle of contrast is operative throughout this work; polarity exists, for instance, in the contrasts between "Die pilgernde Törin" and "Wer ist der Verräter?," between the progressive metamorphosis of "St. Joseph II" and the regressive (negative) "Nicht zu weit." In the appended outline an attempt is made to indicate schematically the relationship between the various novellas (see pp. 144–45).

In the three parts of "Das nußbraune Mädchen" the development of the leader of the emigrant group has been delineated in all its essential details, and here the family concept is never absent. As a future leader of a large metamorphosis of the family, Lenardo must himself establish a family with his Nachodine—"Liebe aus Gewissen" (love as a matter of conscience)—and in the process observe the *Volk*-metamorphosis of the family among the Swiss mountain weavers, which in turn is to be a model for his future community in America.

It will be recalled how Hegel made the education of the young one of the prime responsibilities of the family. It is almost as if Goethe were following the philosopher's outline here; in the conversations with Montan on the mountain and in the pedagogical province this side of the family's activities is expounded. Following Hegel's theories further, a second important area is the management of family property, and here again, in "Der Mann von funfzig Jahren" Goethe seems to be following the philosopher in dealing with the same topic.

And then the negative examples (regressive metamorphoses) are a significant element in the construction of the novel. "Nicht zu weit" negates, so to speak, the blood-related family; "Die gefährliche Wette" does the same for the non-blood-related families. "Die neue Melusine" shows the man unsuited to found a family. How *Steigerung* can operate in human affairs plays a much smaller role, but in the entourage of (and as a result of the influence of) Makarie it is of great importance.

Of all the principles derived from his scientific work that Goethe employed in the novel, the real surprise is the importance of the series. It was not too startling that the family should play a role, since it had been variously mentioned in the literature. What was quite unexpected was the extent and degree to which it was fundamental in the structure of the novel, as has been shown in the foregoing examination. Similarly, neither the important roles of the *Urphänomen* and *Metamorphose*, nor the roles of polarity and *Steigerung*, were completely surprising.

Previous commentary, however, has left one unprepared for the prevalence of the Goethean series everywhere. This is probably due in part to the habit that is all too easy to fall into, namely, that of ignoring the collections of aphorisms entirely out of embarrassment as to how to understand them. Properly understood, however, as kernels of either conversations or of narratives, and then joined to the

CONCLUSION

whole of the novel as Goethe intended, together with all the other series in the novel, they give one the feeling of peering through transparent layers of the work that go on and on. It is somewhat like the repeated mirrored reflections that Goethe studied and that have been referred to above; one gets the impression that they will eventually reach a vanishing point, but they never quite seem to. One gets a dizzy sensation looking for it, and is forced to recall Montan's remark about how real pleasure exists only when one first has a dizzy feeling (p. 31).[1] There is a fundamental difference however in the fact that in the mirrored reflections it is one and the same item that is repeated ad infinitum, while in the transparent stack of series, so to speak, each one is independent, different, individual and important to the whole, whether near the eye or dizzyingly distant.

In the *Wanderjahre*, then, are to be seen innovations on top of innovations, thanks largely to Goethe the pantheist's use of principles gleaned from his scientific research and then used to organize his creative work. The result is a novel which breaks the old mold and sets a new standard.

OUTLINE

RELATIONSHIPS OF NARRATIVE INSERTIONS TO MAIN PLOT AND TO EACH OTHER

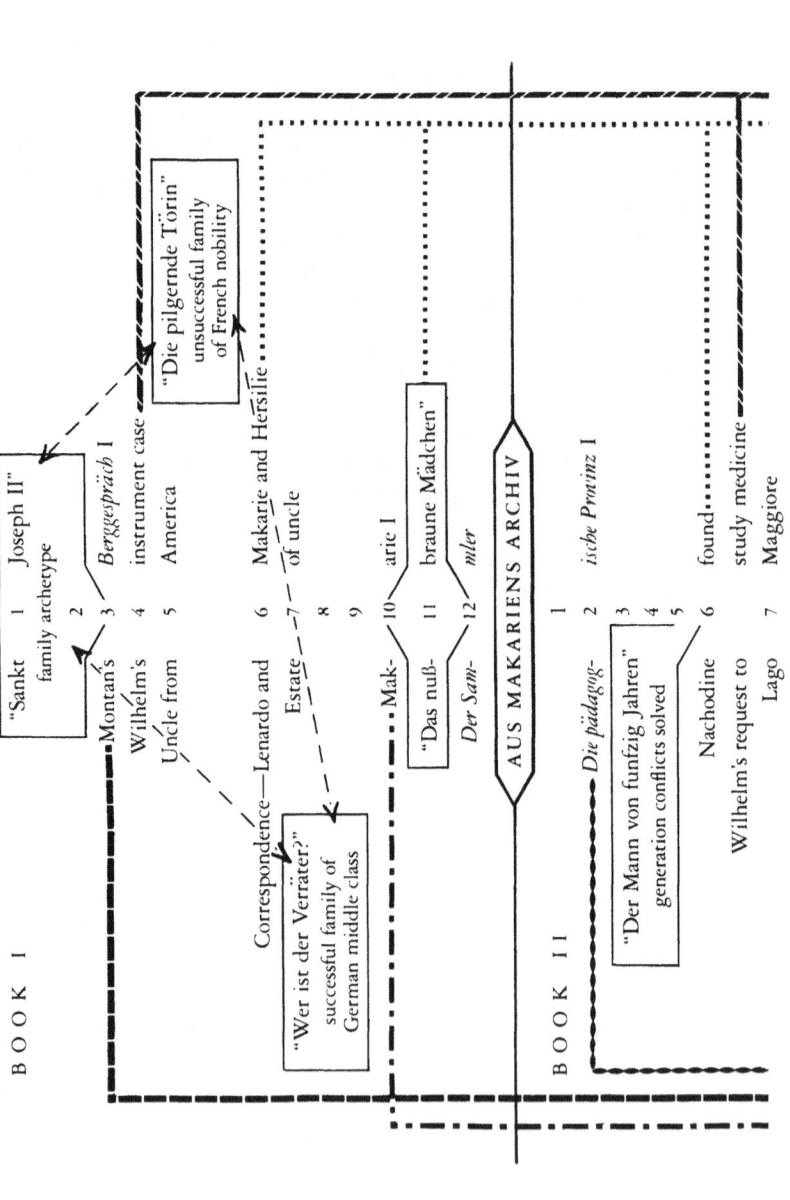

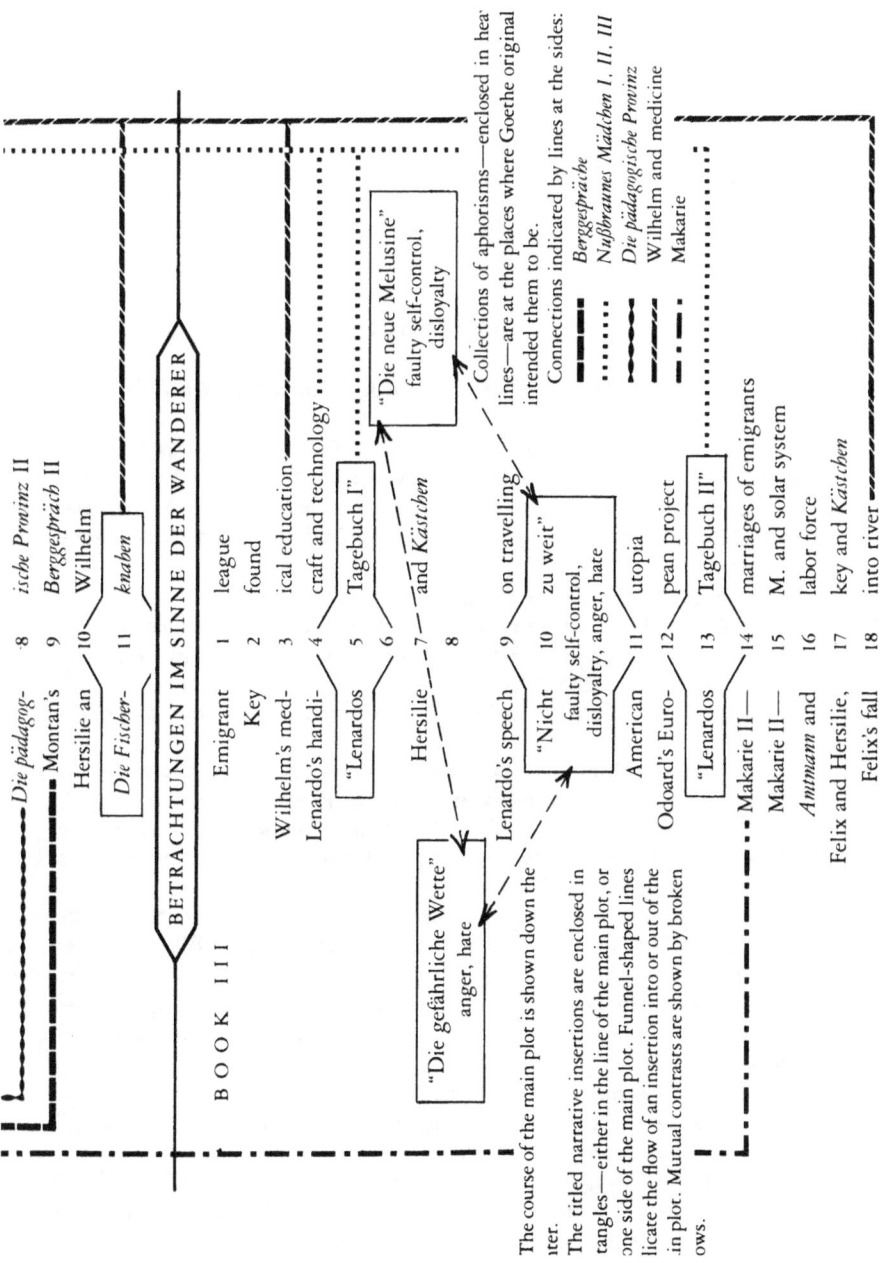

NOTES

PREFACE

1. To Kanzler Müller, 22 January. Hans Gerhard Gräf, *Goethe über seine Dichtungen*, part I, 2:953.
2. Eberhard Sarter, *Zur Technik von Wilhelm Meisters Wanderjahren*; Bernd Peschken, *Entsagung in "Wilhelm Meisters Wanderjahren"*; Anneliese Klingenberg, *Goethes Roman "Wilhelm Meisters Wanderjahre oder die Entsagenden"*; Heidi Gidion, *Zur Darstellungsweise von Goethes "Wilhelm Meisters Wanderjahren."*
3. Emil Staiger, *Goethe* 3: 135, 129, 136.
4. *Goethes Werke*, ed. Erich Trunz. In the following, quotations from the *Wanderjahre* will be cited from vol. 8 of this edition, in parentheses, thus: (p. 261), from other works, volume, then page, thus: (12.420). This edition will be referred to as HA when distinguishing it from other editions.
5. Wilhelm Emrich, "Das Problem der Symbolinterpretation im Hinblick auf Goethes *Wanderjahre*," *Deutsche Vierteljahrsschrift* 26 (1952): 331–52; Robert Hering, *Wilhelm Meister und Faust und ihre Gestaltung im Zeichen der Gottesidee*; Pierre-Paul Sagave, "L'économie et l'homme dans *Les Années de voyage de Wilhelm Meister*," *Etudes Germaniques* 7 (1952):88–104, and in the same journal, "*Les Années de voyage de Wilhelm Meister* et la critique socialiste (1830–1848)" 8 (1953):245–51; Hans S. Reiss, "Bild und Symbol in *Wilhelm Meisters Wanderjahren*," *Studium Generale* 6 (1953):340–48. The present author's fascination with the *Wilhelm Meister* complex dates from a 1952 seminar at the University of Pennsylvania under the late Ernst Jockers.
6. Hans Joachim Schrimpf, *Das Weltbild des späten Goethe*.
7. Claude David, "Goethes *Wanderjahre* als symbolische Dichtung," *Sinn und Form* 8 (1956): 113–28.
8. Herbert Morgan Waidson, "Death by Water, or the Childhood of Wilhelm Meister," *Modern Language Review* 56 (1961):44–53; Friedrich Ohly, "Goethes Ehrfurchten: ein *ordo caritatis*," *Euphorion* 55 (1961): 113–45, 405–48; idem, "Zum Kästchen in Goethes Wanderjahren,"

NOTES

Zeitschrift für deutsches Altertum und deutsche Literatur 91 (1961):255–62; Volker Neuhaus, "Die Archivfiktion in *Wilhelm Meisters Wanderjahren*," *Euphorion* 62 (1968):13–27; Gidion, *Zur Darstellungsweise*, vol. 256; Jane K. Brown, *Goethe's Cyclical Narratives: "Die Unterhaltungen deutscher Ausgewanderten" and "Wilhelm Meisters Wanderjahre."*

THE PROBLEM OF FORM

1. Eduard Spranger, "Der psychologische Perspektivismus im Roman," *Jahrbuch des freien deutschen Hochstifts*, p. 89.
2. Eduard Spranger, "*Wilhelm Meisters Wanderjahre*," *Inselschiff* (1942), p. 223.
3. Brown, *Goethe's Cyclical Narratives*, p. 119.
4. Ibid., p. 98.
5. Arthur Henkel, *Entsagung: Eine Studie zu Goethes Altersroman*, pp. 156–58.
6. To Rochlitz, 28 July 1829 (this and the following are in Gräf, *Goethe*); to Zelter, 5 June 1829 and 24 May 1827; to Sulpiz Boisserée, 2 Sept. 1829.
7. *Goethes Werke*, Weimarer Ausgabe, cited as WA, then division (*Abteilung* I, II, III, IV), then volume and page. Here the following references apply: WA IV 46.66; WA I 36.11; WA IV 46.263; HA 8.8; 9; 11; 15–17; 23; 49; 75; 112; 125; 133; 149; 207; 227; 264; 266–68; 320; 322; 356; 358; 361; 376; 444. Cf. Ehrhard Bahr, *Die Ironie im Spätwerk Goethes*, p. 88.
8. 18 Jan. 1825; Gräf, *Goethe* I, 2:1011.
9. David, "Goethes Wanderjahre," p. 116; Manfred Karnick, "*Wilhelm Meisters Wanderjahre," oder die Kunst des Mittelbaren*, p. 8.
10. Wilhelm Emrich, "Die Erzählkunst des 20. Jahrhunderts und ihr geschichtlicher Sinn," in *Protest und Verheissung*, p. 181.
11. Hermann Broch, "James Joyce und die Gegenwart," in *Dichten und Erkennen, Essays I*, p. 206.
12. Karnick, "*Wilhelm Meisters Wanderjahre*," p. 175.
13. *Goethes sämtliche Werke*, Jubiläumsausgabe, vol. 39, pp. 317–18. Cited hereafter as Jub. with volume and page: Jub. 39.317–18.
14. Ibid., pp. 323, 330.
15. Ibid., pp. 259–61.
16. Cf. A. G. Steer, *Goethe's Social Philosophy*, pp. 12–20.
17. A. B. Wachsmuth, "Goethes naturwissenschaftliches Denken im Spiegel seiner Dichtungen seit 1790," in *Geeinte Zwienatur*, pp. 244–66.

18. Gräf, *Goethe* I, 1:389.
19. WA I 28.356.

THE NARRATIVE INSERTIONS

1. Gertrud Haupt, *Goethes Novellen "Sankt Joseph der Zweite," "Die pilgernde Törin," "Wer ist der Verräter?"*; Emil Krüger, *Die Novellen in Goethes "Wilhelm Meisters Wanderjahren"*; Deli Fischer-Hartmann, *Die innere Einheit in Goethes Roman "Wilhelm Meisters Wanderjahre, oder die Entsagenden"*; Ernst Friedrich von Monroy, "Zur Form der Novelle in *Wilhelm Meisters Wanderjahre*," *Germanisch-Romanische Monatsschrift* 31 (1943):1–17; Waidson, "Death by Water," pp. 44–53; Brown, *Goethe's Cyclical Narratives*.
2. H. A. Korff, *Geist der Goethezeit* 4:644; Spranger, "Wilhelm Meisters Wanderjahre," p. 209.
3. Henkel, *Ensagung*, p. 81.
4. Klingenberg, *Goethes Roman*, p. 127.
5. Ferdinand Gregorovius, *Göthes "Wilhelm Meister" in seinen sozialistischen Elementen entwickelt*, p. 88.
6. Joseph Kunz, *Die deutsche Novelle zwischen Klassik und Romantik*, pp. 25–29.
7. Peschken, *Entsagung*, p. 84; Eric Blackall, "Wilhelm Meister's Pious Pilgrimage," *German Life and Letters* 18 (1964–65):250.
8. 29 Jan. 1827. Gräf, *Goethe* 1:232.
9. Ibid., 951.
10. Ibid., 958.
11. Gregorovius, *Göthes Wilhelm Meister*, pp. 88–90.
12. Sarter, *Zur Technik*, p. 37.
13. Hering, *Wilhelm Meister und Faust*, p. 233.
14. Ehrhard Bahr, *Die Ironie im Spätwerk Goethes ". . . diese sehr ernsten Scherze . . .,"* p. 94.
15. Ehrhard Bahr, "Goethe's *Wanderjahre* as an Experimental Novel," in *New Views of the European Novel*, p. 61.
16. Klingenberg, *Goethes Roman*, p. 160.
17. Henkel, *Entsagung*, p. 76.
18. Neuhaus, "Die Archivfiktion," p. 14; Kunz, *Die deutsche Novelle*, p. 27.
19. Gidion, *Zur Darstellungsweise*, p. 42. Peschken calls the phenomenon "Erzählweise," *Entsagung*, p. 218.
20. Kunz, *Die deutsche Novelle*, p. 28.
21. Gidion, *Zur Darstellungsweise*, p. 12; Henkel, *Entsagung*, p. 76.
22. Henkel, *Entsagung*, p. 76.

23. Eugen Wolff, "Die ursprüngliche Gestalt von *Wilhelm Meisters Wanderjahren,*" *Goethejahrbuch* 34 (1913):169. Similarly Emrich, "Das Problem der Symbolinterpretation," p. 348.
24. WA I 18.190.
25. HA 8.581.
26. WA IV 43.83.
27. David, "Goethes Wanderjahre," p. 125.
28. Korff, *Geist der Goethezeit* 4:644; similarly Hans Reiss, *Goethes Romane*, p. 208; cf. also Karl Schlechta, *Goethes "Wilhelm Meister,"* pp. 176–202.
29. WA IV 46.66.
30. WA I 25.115.
31. WA IV 36.110.

THE FAMILY AS ARCHETYPE AND METAMORPHOSIS

1. Cf. Pierre-Paul Sagave,"*Les Années de voyage*," pp. 245–51.
2. Used here is the edition of Alfred Bäumer (Jena, 1927), particularly Bäumer's introduction and then paragraphs 258, 166, 161, 167, 170, 173, and 181.
3. See Steer, *Goethe's Social Philosophy*, pp. 9–21; idem, "Goethes 'St. Rochus-Fest zu Bingen,'" in *Jahrbuch des freien deutschen Hochstifts* (1965), pp. 186–236.
4. 7 October 1820; WA IV 33.295; see also Werner Kahle, "Zum Hegel-Bild in den Briefen Goethes," in *Goethe Jahrbuch* (1974), pp. 25–32.
5. 13 April 1821; WA IV 34.191.
6. 14 November 1827; WA IV 43.168.
7. Karl Rosenkrantz, *Goethe und seine Werke*, p. 390.
8. Gregorovius, *Göthes "Wilhelm Meister."* See also Hering, *Wilhelm Meister und Faust*, p. 423.
9. Ibid., pp. 99, 122, 129.
10. Alexander Jung, *Goethes "Wanderjahre" und die wichtigsten Fragen des 19. Jahrhunderts*, p. 265.
11. Klingenberg, *Goethes Roman*, p. 20.
12. Trunz, HA 8.592. Also idem, "Seelische Kultur," *Deutsche Vierteljahrsschrift* 24 (1950): 233.
13. Gräf, *Goethe I*, 1:193.
14. Thomas Mann, "Goethe and Democracy," *Publications of the English Goethe Society 1949*, p. 14.
15. Henkel, *Entsagung*, p. 146.
16. Peschken, *Entsagung*, p. 165.

17. Gidion, *Zur Darstellungsweise*, p. 213.
18. Trunz, "Seelische Kultur," p. 233.
19. Anna von Hellersberg-Wendriner, "Soziologischer Wandel im Weltbild Goethes," *PMLA* 56 (1941):448.

"SAINT JOSEPH THE SECOND"

1. 10 May; Gräf, *Goethe* I, 2:883.
2. Cf. Gräf, *Goethe* I, 2:889, 702.
3. 2 May 1824; *Goethes Gespräche*, ed. F. von Biedermann, 3:104; Schrimpf, *Weltbild des späten Goethe*, p. 148.
4. Robert Riemann, *Goethes Romantechnik*, p. 53.
5. Sarter, *Zur Technik*, p. 21.
6. Gidion, *Zur Darstellungsweise*, p. 21.
7. Ibid., p. 18.
8. Cf. Helmut Esau, "Die Landschaft in Goethes *Wilhelm Meisters Wanderjahren*," in *Colloquia Germanica* (1973), p. 238.
9. Hering, *Wilhelm Meister und Faust*, p. 241–42.
10. Ibid., p. 242.
11. See also Schrimpf, *Weltbild des späten Goethe*, p. 146.
12. WA I 49.158–59.
13. Christian Schuchardt, *Goethes Kunstsammlungen* 1:196.
14. Gidion, *Zur Darstellungsweise*, p. 20.
15. HA 12: 138–42, 612.
16. Brown, *Goethe's Cyclical Narratives*, p. 34.
17. Steer, "'Rochus-Fest,'" pp. 217–23. See also Ziolkowski, "Die Natur als Nachahmung der Kunst bei Goethe," *passim*.
18. Von Monroy, "Zur Form der Novelle," pp. 7–9.
19. Klingenberg, *Goethes Roman*, p. 31.
20. Brown, *Goethes Cyclical Narratives*, p. 42.
21. Gustav Radbruch, "Wilhelm Meisters sozialistische Sendung," *Gestalten und Gedanken*, p. 98.
22. Haupt, *Goethes Novellen*, p. 181.
23. Schrimpf, *Weltbild des späten Goethe*, p. 269.

"DIE PILGERNDE TÖRIN"

1. Von Monroy, "Zur Form der Novelle," p. 2. He points out that the earthy note characteristic of the Italian or French novella has been replaced by a more sophisticated smoothness.

NOTES

2. Cf. Riemann, *Goethes Romantechnik*, p. 53.
3. WA I 1.192.
4. Henkel, *Entsagung*, p. 82.
5. Klingenberg, *Goethes Roman*, pp. 128–30.
6. Karnick, "*Wilhelm Meisters Wanderjahre*," p. 79.
7. Quoted in part; WA I 25.31–32.

"DAS NUSSBRAUNE MÄDCHEN"

1. Sagave, "L'économie et l'homme," p. 92. He sees the uncle as thoroughly justified, according to the New Testament parable of the talents, in taking from those who have not and giving to those who have; i.e., he sees a secularization of a Christian virtue.
2. Gräf, *Goethe* I, 2:892. 4 Aug.
3. Ibid., p. 900, 19 Nov.
4. Ibid., p. 904, 11 May.
5. Through Herder and Schlosser. Cf. Emil Krüger, *Die Novellen in "Wilhelm Meisters Wanderjahren,"* p. 16.
6. Cf. Eugen Wolff, *Goethes "Wilhelm Meisters Wanderjahre": Ein Novellenkranz*, p. 27.
7. Cf. Peter Horwath, "Zur Namengebung des 'Nußbraunen Mädchens' in Goethes *Wilhelm Meisters Wanderjahren*," *Goethe Jahrbuch* 89 (1972): 300–303.
8. Brown, *Goethe's Cyclical Narratives*, p. 98.
9. WA I 25.210.
10. Cf. A. G. Steer, "The Wound and the Physician in Goethe's *Wilhelm Meister*," in *Studies in German Literature of the 19th and 20th Centuries*, pp. 11–23.
11. Von Monroy, *Zur Form der Novelle*, p. 11.
12. *Goethes sämtliche Werke*, Propyläen-Ausgabe, vol. 34, p. 159. Hereafter referred to as "Prop." with volume and page.
13. Sagave, "L'économie et l'homme," p. 96.
14. Radbruch, "Wilhelm Meisters Sozialistische Sendung," p. 99.
15. Meyer's notes have survived: cf. WA I 25.261–71.
16. HA 8.707.
17. Prop. 34.162.

"WER IST DER VERRÄTER?"

1. Cf. Haupt, *Goethes Novellen*, pp. 70–71.

2. Radbruch, "Wilhelm Meisters sozialistische Sendung," p. 120.
3. Eric A. Blackall, *Goethe and the Novel*, p. 265.
4. Riemann, *Goethes Romantechnik*, p. 53.
5. Haupt, *Goethes Novellen*, p. 72.
6. Brown, *Goethe's Cyclical Narratives*, p. 51.
7. Klingenberg, *Goethes Roman*, p. 138.
8. HA 8.628–29.
9. Von Monroy, *Zur Form der Novelle*, p. 6.
10. Prop. 34.162.
11. Ibid.
12. WA I 25.209–15
13. Cf. L. A. Willoughby, "Literary Relations in the Light of Goethe's Principle of Wiederspiegelung,'" *Comparative Literature* 1 (1949):320; also Ernst Beutler, "Lili: Wiederholte Spiegelungen," *Essays um Goethe* 2 (1947):1.

"DER MANN VON FUNFZIG JAHREN"

1. The title was apparently influenced by Kotzebue's drama, "Der Mann von vierzig Jahren." Gustav Kettner, "Goethes Novelle 'Der Mann von funfzig Jahren,'" *Neue Jahrbücher für das klassische Altertum* 33 (1914): 66–78, has a good account of the *Entstehungsgeschichte*.
2. Prop. 34.78.
3. Cf. Krüger, *Die Novellen*, pp. 23–26; Klingenberg, *Goethes Roman*, p. 134.
4. WA I 25.229–47.
5. Goethe's Gespräche 2:506.
6. WA I 25.246–47.
7. Benno von Wiese, *Die deutsche Novelle von Goethe bis Kafka* 2:31.
8. WA I 25.245.
9. There is no question but that Goethe's own attraction to much younger women played a role here; for instance, 1807—Bettina Brentano (Goethe 58); 1807—Minna Herzlieb (Goethe 58); 1808—Sylvie von Ziegesaar (Goethe 59); 1814–15—Marianne von Willemer (Goethe 65–66); 1823—Ulrike von Levetzow (Goethe 74!).
10. WA I 25.246.
11. WA IV 19.479–81.
12. Henkel, *Entsagung*, p. 103.

WILHELM'S PREHISTORY

1. Waidson, "Death by Water," pp. 44–53.
2. Cf. Steer, "The Wound and the Physician," p. 13.
3. Peschken, *Entsagung*, p. 96. He sees part of the complexities here, including one instance of framing, but his method of analysis—simply numbering the elements as *Erzählfragmente*—seems to have obscured his view.
4. Apparently Goethe liked this comparison; he used it earlier in *Kunst und Altertum am Rhein und Main* in connection with Sulpiz Boisserée in 1816; 13.142–43, 613.
5. Brown, *Goethe's Cyclical Narratives*, p. 117.
6. Radbruch, "Wilhelm Meisters sozialistische Sendung," pp. 90–91, establishes an interesting connection between the sentence quoted and the last of Goethe's Strassburg theses, 1771.

"DIE NEUE MELUSINE"

1. Gräf, *Goethe* I, 2:876 (4 February).
2. Severin Rüttgers, ed., *Deutsche Volksbücher*, pp. 215–41 and 621.
3. Gonthier-Louis Fink, "Goethes 'Neue Melusine' und die Elementargeister," *Goethe* 21 (1959):140–51.

"DIE GEFÄHRLICHE WETTE"

1. Riemann, *Goethes Romantechnik*, p. 56.
2. Gregorovius, *Göthes Wilhelm Meister*, p. 192.
3. Klingenberg, *Goethes Roman*, p. 141.
4. Wolff, *Novellenkranz*, p. 30.
5. Brown, *Goethe's Cyclical Narratives*, p. 105.
6. Klingenberg, *Goethes Roman*, p. 142.
7. Oskar Seidlin, "*Melusine* in der Spiegelung der *Wanderjahre*," in *Aspekte der Goethezeit*, p. 151.

"NICHT ZU WEIT"

1. Gidion, *Zur Darstellungsweise*, pp. 53, 54.
2. Riemann, *Goethes Romantechnik*, p. 55.

3. Von Monroy, *Zur Form der Novelle*, p. 13; Henkel, *Entsagung*, p. 58.
4. Hildebrandt, *Goethe: Seine Weisheit im Gesamtwerk*, p. 492.
5. Beutler, *Essays um Goethe*, pp. 103–8; Heinrich Deiters, "Goethes Gedanken über Jugenderziehung in *Wilhelm Meisters Wanderjahren*," *Goethe* 22 (1960):31.
6. Sagave, "L'économie et l'homme," p. 97; Hering, *Wilhelm Meister und Faust*, p. 301.
7. Arndt, Karl J. R., "The Harmony Society and *Wilhelm Meisters Wanderjahre*," *Comparative Literature* 10 (1958):198.
8. Von Monroy, *Zur Form der Novelle*, pp. 14–15; Brown, *Goethe's Cyclical Narratives*, p. 171.
9. Prop. 34.145.
10. Hildebrandt, *Goethe*, pp. 485–91.
11. Eva Alexander Meyer, *Goethes "Wilhelm Meister,"* also notes parallels to Odoard's tale, p. 198.

THE NONTITLED NARRATIVE INSERTIONS

1. See above, notes 6, 7, and 8 in "Narrative Insertions."
2. Prop. 34.26.
3. Otto Kohlmeyer, *Die pädagogische Provinz*; Karl Jungmann, "Die pädagogische Provinz in *Wilhelm Meisters Wanderjahren: Eine Quellenstudie*," *Euphorion* 14 (1907): 274–87, 517–33; Ernst Beutler, "Die vierfache Ehrfurcht," *Modern Language Quarterly* 10 (1949):259–63; Harold Jantz, "Die Ehrfurchten in Goethes *Wilhelm Meister*," *Euphorion* 48 (1954):1–18; Ohly, "Goethes Ehrfurcht," pp. 113–45, 405–48.
4. Quoted by Klingenberg, *Goethes Roman*, p. 57.
5. Cf. Reiss, *Goethes Romane*, p. 224.
6. Goethe had reread Cervantes's stories as he prepared to start on the *Wanderjahre*, 2 February 1801. The irony here makes one wonder if he was recalling the place in *Don Quixote II* where the knight meets people who have read part I! (Pt. II, 14.)
7. Cf. Meyer, *Goethes Wilhelm Meister*, p. 198.
8. See above, p. 12.

APHORISMS, MAXIMS AND REFLECTIONS

1. Max Wundt, "'Aus Makariens Archiv': Zur Entstehung der Aphorismensammlung," *Germanisch-Romanische Monatsschrift* 7 (1915): 177–84.

2. Erich Trunz, "Die *Wanderjahre* als 'Hauptgeschäft' im Winterhalbjahr 1828/1829," in *Natur und Idee*, pp. 254–56.
   3. Paul Stöcklein, epilogue to *Goethes Werke*, 9:744.
   4. Reiss, "*Wilhelm Meisters Wanderjahre*," pp. 55–56.
   5. Gidion, *Zur Darstellungsweise*, p. 138.
   6. Gerhart Baumann, *Maxime und Reflexion als Stilform bei Goethe*, p. 69.
   7. Sarter, *Zur Technik*, p. 33.
   8. Stöcklein, *Goethes Werke*, p. 738.
   9. Wilhelm Flitner, "Aus Makariens Archiv: Ein Beispiel Goethescher Spruchkomposition," *Goethe-Kalendar* (1943), pp. 116–74.
   10. Gerhard Neumann, *Ideenparadiese: Untersuchungen zur Aphoristik bei Lichtenberg, Novalis, Friedrich Schlegel und Goethe*, p. 724.
   11. Ibid., p. 673.
   12. Ibid., p. 726.
   13. Ibid., p. 704.

THE GOETHEAN SERIES

   1. Jub. 39.179–202.
   2. Jub. 39.182.
   3. Rudolf Magnus, *Goethe as a Scientist*, pp. 59, 223, 225, *et passim*.
   4. Jub. 39.259–95.
   5. Steer, *Goethe's Social Philosophy*, pp. 12–30.
   6. Gräf, *Goethe* I, 2:985; 7 Sept.
   7. To Wieland, 21 Nov. (?), 1809. Gräf, *Goethe* I, 1:422.

THE *WANDERJAHRE* AS *SCHLÜSSELROMAN*

   1. See Georg Schneider, *Die Schlüsselliteratur*.
   2. For instance, Bahr, *Die Ironie im Spätwerk Goethes*, pp. 111–13; Paul Böckmann, "Voraussetzungen der zyklischen Erzählform in *Wilhelm Meisters Wanderjahren*," *Festschrift für Detlev W. Schumann*, pp. 141–44; Wilhelm Emrich, "Das Problem der Symbolinterpretation im Hinblick auf Goethes *Wanderjahre*," *Deutsche Vierteljahrsschrift* 26 (1952):331–52; idem, "Symbolinterpretation und Mythenforschung," *Euphorion* 47 (1953):38–67; Henkel, *Entsagung*, p. 89; Hering, *Wilhelm Meister und Faust*, pp. 369–70; Klingenberg, *Goethes Roman*; Meyer, *Goethes "Wilhelm Meister,"* p. 144; Ohly, "Zum Kästchen," pp. 255–59.
   3. Cf. Emrich, "Problem der Symbolinterpretation," p. 47.
   4. J. J. Bachofen, *Gräbersymbolik der Alten*, pp. 314–15.

5. Ohly, "Zum Kästchen"; idem, "Goethes Ehrfurchten," pp. 113–45, 405–48.
6. Blackall, *Goethe and the Novel*, p. 258, where he also sees a sexual symbolism in the key.
7. Gerhard Femmel, ed., *Corpus der Goethezeichnungen* 6A: 65, 66.
8. WA I 53.198.
9. Ibid.
10. Emrich, "Problem der Symbolinterpretation," p. 348; Ohly, "Goethes Ehrfurchten," p. 42.
11. Ohly, "Zum Kästchen."
12. Femmel, *Goethezeichnungen* 3A:81.
13. *Pauly-Wissova*, s. v. "Die Eleusinischen Weihen"; Alfred Körte, "Zu den Eleusinischen Mysterien," *Archiv für Religionswissenschaft* 18 (1915):116–26; M. P. Nilsson, "Die Eleusinischen Gottheiten," *Archiv für Religionswissenschaft* 32 (1935):79–141; *Reallexikon für Antike und Christentum*, s. v. "Eleusis."

CONCLUSION

1. Blackall, *Goethe and the Novel*, p. 226.

BIBLIOGRAPHY

GOETHE'S WORKS

Goethes Werke. Edited by Erich Trunz. 14 vols. Hamburg, 1950.
Goethes sämtliche Werke. Jubiläumsausgabe. 41 vols. Stuttgart, 1904.
Goethes Werke. Weimarer Ausgabe. 143 vols. Weimar, 1890.
Goethes sämtliche Werke. Propyläen-Ausgabe. Berlin, 1926.
Goethes Gespräche. Edited by F. von Biedermann. 5 vols. Leipzig, 1910.

SECONDARY SOURCES

Arndt, Karl J. R. "The Harmony Society and *Wilhelm Meisters Wanderjahre.*" *Comparative Literature* 10 (1958):193–202.
Bachofen, J. J. *Gräbersymbolik der Alten.* Basel, 1925.
Bahr, Ehrhard. "Goethe's *Wanderjahre* as an Experimental Novel." *New Views of the European Novel*, edited by R. G. Collins. Winnipeg, 1972.
———. "Die Ironie im Spätwerk Goethes '. . . diese sehr ernsten Scherze . . .'." Berlin, 1972.
Bastian, Hans Jürgen. "Die Gesellschaftsproblematik in Goethes Roman *Wilhelm Meisters Wanderjahre oder die Entsagenden.*" *Weimarer Beiträge* 5/6 (1966):984–86.
———. "Makrostruktur in *Wilhelm Meisters Wanderjahren.*" *Weimarer Beiträge* 9/10 (1968):634.
———. "Zum Menschenbild des späten Goethe: Interpretation von St. Joseph der Zweite." *Weimarer Berträge* 12 (1966):471–88.
Bäumler, Alfred, ed. *Hegels Schriften zur Gesellschaftsphilosophie.* Part I, *Philosophie des Geistes und Rechtsphilosophie* (1821). Jena, 1927.
Bauer, George-Karl. "Makarie." *Germanisch-Romanische Monatsschrift* 25 (1937):178–97.
Baumann, Gerhart. *Maxime und Reflexion als Stilform bei Goethe.* Ph.D. dissertation, University of Karlsruhe, 1949.
Becker, Henrik. "Eine Quelle zu Goethes 'Neuer Melusine.'" *Zeitschrift für deutsche Philologie* 52 (1927):150–51.

Berthau, Friedrich. *Goethe und seine Beziehung zur schweizerischen Baumwoll-Industrie, nebst dem Nachweise, daß unter Frau Susanne, der Fabrikantenfrau in "Wilhelm Meisters Wanderjahren" Frau Barbara Schulthess von Zürich zu verstehen ist*. Wetzikon, 1888.
Beutler, Ernst. *Essays um Goethe*. 6th ed. Bremen, 1957.
―――. "Die vierfache Ehrfurcht." *Modern Language Quarterly* 10 (1949):259–63.
Blackall, Eric A. *Goethe and the Novel*. Ithaca, New York, 1976.
―――. "Wilhelm Meister's Pious Pilgrimage." *German Life and Letters* 18 (1964–65):246–51.
Böckmann, Paul. "Voraussetzungen der zyklischen Erzählform in *Wilhelm Meisters Wanderjahren*." In *Festschrift für Detlev W. Schumann*, edited by Albert R. Schmidt. Munich, 1970.
Broch, Hermann. "James Joyce und die Gegenwart." In *Dichten und Erkennen, Essays I*, edited by Hanna Arendt. Zürich, 1955.
Brown, Jane K. *Goethe's Cyclical Narratives: "Die Unterhaltungen deutscher Ausgewanderten" and "Wilhelm Meisters Wanderjahre."* Chapel Hill, 1975.
Dahl, Hermann. "Goethes sozialer Staat." *Tat: Wege zum freien Menschentum* 11 (1919–20):912–17.
David, Claude. "Goethes *Wanderjahre* als symbolische Dichtung." *Sinn und Form* 8 (1956):113–28.
Deiters, Heinrich. "Goethes Gedanken über Jugenderziehung in *Wilhelm Meisters Wanderjahren*." *Goethe: Neue Folge des Jahrbuchs der Goethegesellschaft* 22 (1960):21–38.
Dzialas, Ingrid. "Auffassung und Darstellung der Elemente bei Goethe." In *Germanische Studien* 216. Berlin, 1939.
Emrich, Wilhelm. "Das Problem der Symbolinterpretation im Hinblick auf Goethes *Wanderjahre*." *Deutsche Vierteljahrsschrift* 26(1952):331–52.
―――. "Symbolinterpretation und Mythenforschung." *Euphorion* 47 (1953):38–67.
―――. "Die Erzählkunst des 20. Jahrhunderts und ihr geschichtlicher Sinn." *Protest und Verheißung*. Frankfurt/M., 1968.
Esau, Helmut. "Die Landschaft in Goethes *Wilhelm Meisters Wanderjahren*." *Colloquia Germanica* (1973), pp. 234–49.
Falkenheim, Hugo. *Goethe und Hegel*. Tübingen, 1934.
Femmel, Gerhard, ed. *Corpus der Goethezeichnungen*. 7 vols. Leipzig, 1970.
Fink, Gonthier-Louis. "Goethes 'Neue Melusine' und die Elementargeister." *Goethe: Neue Folge des Jahrbuchs der Goethegesellschaft* 21 (1959): 140–51.
―――. "Die Auseinandersetzung mit der Tradition in *Wilhelm Meisters Wanderjahre*." *Recherches Germaniques*. Université des Sciences Humaines de Strasbourg. Vol. 5, n. d.

Fischer-Hartmann, Deli. "Die innere Einheit in Goethes Roman *Wilhelm Meisters Wanderjahre, oder die Entsagenden.*" Ph.D. dissertation, University of Freiburg, 1941.

Flitner, Wilhelm. "Goethes Erziehungsgedanken in *Wilhelm Meisters Wanderjahren.*" *Goethe* 12 (1960):39–53.

———. *Goethe im Spätwerk.* Hamburg, 1947.

———. "'Aus Makariens Archiv': Ein Beispiel Goethescher Spruchkomposition." *Goethe-Kalendar* (1943), pp. 116–74.

———. Epilogue to *Wilhelm Meisters Wanderjahren.* Munich: Deutscher Taschenbuchverlag, 1962.

Gidion, Heidi. *Zur Darstellungsweise von Goethes "Wilhelm Meisters Wanderjahren."* Göttingen, 1969.

Gräf, Hans Gerhard. *Goethe über seine Dichtungen.* 9 vols. Darmstadt, 1968.

Gregorovius, Ferdinand Adolf. *Göthes "Wilhelm Meister" in seinen sozialistischen Elementen entwickelt.* Königsberg, 1849.

Haas, Gerhard. *Studien zur Form des Essays und zu seinen Vorformen im Roman.* Tübingen, 1966.

Hahn, Karl-Heinz. "Goethes Verhältnis zur Romantik." *Goethe* 29 (1967):43–64.

Haupt, Gertrud. *Goethes Novellen "Sankt Joseph der Zweite," "Die pilgernde Törin," "Wer ist der Verräter?"* Ph.D. dissertation, University of Greifswald, 1913.

Hellersberg-Wendriner, Anna. "America in the World View of the Aged Goethe." *Germanic Review* 14 (1939):270–76.

———. "Soziologischer Wandel im Weltbild Goethes," *PMLA* 56 (1941):447–65.

Henkel, Arthur. *Entsagung: Eine Studie zu Goethes Altersroman*, 2nd ed. Tübingen, 1964.

Hering, Robert. *"Wilhelm Meister" und "Faust" und ihre Gestaltung im Zeichen der Gottesidee.* Frankfurt/M., 1952.

Hildebrandt, Kurt. *Goethe: Seine Weisheit im Gesamtwerk.* 3rd ed. Leipzig, 1942.

Horvath, Peter. "Zur Namengebung des 'Nußbraunen Mädchens' in *Wilhelm Meisters Wanderjahren.*" *Goethe Jahrbuch* 89 (1972):297–304.

Jantz, Harold. "Die Ehrfurchten in Goethe's *Wilhelm Meister.*" *Euphorion* 48 (1954):1–18.

Jessen, Myra R. "Spannungsgefüge und Stilisierung in den Goetheschen Novellen." *PMLA* 55 (1940):445–71.

Jung, Alexander. *Göthes "Wanderjahre" und die wichtigsten Fragen des 19. Jahrhunderts.* Mainz, 1854.

Jungmann, Karl. "Die pädagogische Provinz in *Wilhelm Meisters Wanderjahren*: eine Quellenstudie." *Euphorion* 14 (1907): 274–87, 517–33.

Kahle, Werner. "Zum Hegel-Bild in den Briefen Goethes." *Goethe Jahrbuch* 91 (1974):25–32.

Karnick, Manfred. *"Wilhelm Meisters Wanderjahre," oder die Kunst des Mittelbaren*. Munich, 1968.

Kern, Otto. "Die Eleusinischen Weihen." In *Paulys Enzyklopädie der klassischen Altertumswissenschaft* 16 (1935): cols. 1211–1314.

Kettner, Gustav. "Goethes Novelle 'Der Mann von funfzig Jahren.'" *Neue Jahrbücher für das klassische Altertum* 33 (1914):66–78.

Klingenberg, Anneliese. *Goethes Roman "Wilhelm Meisters Wanderjahre oder die Entsagenden."* Berlin, 1972.

Kohlmeyer, Otto. *Die pädagogische Provinz*. Langensalza, 1923.

Korff, H. A. *Geist der Goethezeit*. 5 vols. Leipzig, 1953.

Körte, Alfred. "Zu den Eleusinischen Mysterien." *Archiv für Religionswissenschaft* 18 (1915):116–26.

Krogmann, Willy. "Goethes dramatischer Entwurf 'Der Mann von funfzig Jahren.'" *Archiv für das Studium der neueren Sprachen* 314 (1940):73f.

Krüger, Emil. *Die Novellen in "Wilhelm Meisters Wanderjahren."* Kiel, 1926.

Küntzel, Gerhard. "*Wilhelm Meisters Wanderjahre* in der ersten Fassung 1821." *Goethe: Viermonatsschrift der Goethegesellschaft* 3 (1938):3–39.

Kunz, Joseph. *Die deutsche Novelle zwischen Klassik und Romantik*. Berlin, 1966.

Leipoldt, J. "Eleusis." *Reallexikon für Antike und Christentum* 4 (1959): cols. 1100–1103.

Loeb, Ernst. "Makarie und Faust." *Zeitschrift für Deutsche Philologie* 88 (1969–70):583–97.

Magnus, Rudolf. *Goethe as a Scientist*. Translated by Gunther Schmid. New York, 1949.

Mann, Thomas. "Goethe and Democracy." *Publications of the English Goethe Society 1949*. London, 1949.

Mannack, Eberhard. *Raumdarstellung und Realitätsbezug in Goethes epischer Dichtung*. Frankfurt/M., 1972.

Marache, Maurice. *Le Symbole dans la pensée et l'oeuvre de Goethe*. Paris, 1960.

Meyer, Eva Alexander. *Goethes "Wilhelm Meister."* Munich, 1947.

Michel, Karl. "Die Entsagung: Vier Studien zu Goethe." *Sinn und Form* 20 (1968):686–96.

Mommsen, Katharina. "Goethes Vorstellung von einer idealen Lesergemeinde." *Seminar* 10 (1974):1–8.

von Monroy, Ernst Friedrich. "Zur Form der Novelle in *Wilhelm Meisters Wanderjahre*." *Germanisch-Romanische Monatsschrift* 31 (1943):1–17.

Neuhaus, Volker. "Die Archivfiktion in *Wilhelm Meisters Wanderjahren*." *Euphorion* 62 (1968):13–27.

Neumann, Gerhard. *Ideenparadiese: Untersuchungen zur Aphoristik bei Lichtenberg, Novalis, Friedrich Schlegel und Goethe*. Munich, 1976.
Nilsson, Martin P. "Die Eleusinischen Gottheiten." *Archiv für Religionswissenschaft* 32 (1935):79–141.
Nitschke, Otfried. *Goethes pädagogische Provinz*. Würzburg, 1937.
Ohly, Friedrich. "Goethes Ehrfurchten—ein *ordo caritatis*." *Euphorion* 55 (1961): 113–45, 405–48.
―――. "Zum Kästchen in Goethes *Wanderjahren*." *Zeitschrift für deutsches Altertum und deutsche Literatur* 91 (1961):225–59.
Oppel, Horst. *Morphologische Literaturwissenschaft*. Darmstadt, 1967.
Peschken, Bernd. *Entsagung in "Wilhelm Meisters Wanderjahren."* Bonn, 1968.
Petritis, Aivars. *Die Gestaltung der Personen in Goethes "Wilhelm Meisters Lehjahren" und "Wilhelm Meisters Wanerjahren."* Ph.D. dissertation, University of Bonn, 1967.
Raabe, August. "Das Dämonische in den *Wanderjahren*." *Goethe: Vierteljahrsschrift der Goethegesellschaft* 1 (1936):119–27.
Radbruch, Gustav. "Wilhelm Meisters sozialistische Sendung." In *Gestalten und Gedanken*. Leipzig, 1944.
Rausch, Jürgen. "Lebensstufen in Goethes *Wilhelm Meister*." *Deutsche Vierteljahrsschrift* 20 (1942):65–114.
Reiss, Hans S. "Bild und Symbol in *Wilhelm Meisters Wanderjahren*." *Studium Generale* 6 (1953):340–48.
―――. *Goethes Romane*. Bern, 1963.
―――. "*Wilhelm Meisters Wanderjahre*: Der Weg von der ersten zur zweiten Fassung." *Deutsche Vierteljahrsschrift* 39 (1965):35–57.
Remak, Henry H. H. "Amerikanischer Geist in Goethes *Wilhelm Meisters Wanderjahre*." In *Festschrift für Werner Neuse*. Edited by Herbert Lederer and Joachim Seyppel. Berlin, 1967.
Riemann, Robert. *Goethes Romantechnik*. Leipzig, 1902.
Röder, Gerda. *Glück und glückliches Ende im deutschen Bildungsroman*. Munich, 1968.
Rosenkranz, Karl. *Goethe und seine Werke*. 2nd ed. Königsberg, 1847.
Ruhtenberg, Grete. "Der Schlüssel in *Wilhelm Meisters Wanderjahre*." *Erziehungskunst* 25 (1961):370–73.
Ruttgers, Severin, ed. *Deutsche Volksbücher*. Leipzig, n. d.
Sarter, Eberhard. *Zur Technik von "Wilhelm Meisters Wanderjahren."* Berlin, 1914.
Sagave, Pierre-Paul. "*Les années de voyage de Wilhelm Meister* et la critique socialiste (1830–1848)." *Etudes Germaniques* 8 (1953):245–51.
―――. "L'économie et l'homme dans *Les années de voyage de Wilhelm*

Meister." *Etudes Germaniques* 7 (1952):88–104.
Schädel, Christian H. *Metamorphose und Erscheinungsformen des Menschseins in "Wilhelm Meisters Wanderjahren."* Marburg, 1969.
Schlechta, Karl. *Goethes Wilhelm Meister.* Frankfurt/M., 1953.
Schmidlin, Bruno. *Das Motiv des Wanderns bei Goethe.* Winterthur, 1963.
Schneider, Georg. *Die Schlüsselliteratur.* 2 vols. Stuttgart, 1951.
Schrimpf, Hans Joachim. *Das Weltbild des späten Goethe.* Stuttgart, 1956.
Schuchardt, Christian. *Goethes Kunstsammlungen.* 3 vols. Jena, 1848.
Seidlin, Oskar. "*Melusine* in der Spiegelung der *Wanderjahre.*" In *Aspekte der Goethezeit.* Edited by Stanley A. Corngold et al. Göttingen, 1977.
Spranger, Eduard. *Goethes Weltanschauung.* Inselverlag, 1946.
———. "Der psychologische Perspektivismus im Roman." *Jahrbuch des freien deutschen Hochstifts.* Edited by Ernst Beutler. Frankfurt/M., 1930.
———. "Die sittliche Astrologie der Makarie in *Wilhelm Meisters Wanderjahren.*" In *Goethe: Seine geistige Welt.* Tübingen, 1967.
———. "*Wilhelm Meisters Wanderjahre.*" In *Inselschiff*, 1942.
Staiger, Emil. *Goethe.* 3 vols. Zürich, 1952–59.
Steer, A. G. *Goethe's Social Philosophy.* Chapel Hill, 1955.
———. "Goethes 'St. Rochus-Fest zu Bingen.'" *Jahrbuch des freien deutschen Hochstifts* (1965), pp. 186–236.
———. "The Wound and the Physician in Goethe's Wilhelm Meister." *Studies in German Literature of the 19th and 20th Centuries.* Chapel Hill, 1970.
Stöcklein, Paul. *Goethes Werke.* Epilogue to volume 9. Zürich, 1949.
———. *Wege zum späten Goethe.* Hamburg, 1949.
Thalmann, Marianne. *J. W. von Goethe: "Der Mann von funfzig Jahren."* Wien, 1948.
Trunz, Erich. "Seelische Kultur." *Deutsche Vierteljahrsschrift* 24 (1950): 214–43.
———. "Die *Wanderjahre* als 'Hauptgeschäft' im Winterhalbjahr 1828/1829." *Natur und Idee.* Edited by Helmut Holzhauer. Weimar, 1966.
Urzidil, Johannes. *Das Glück der Gegenwart: Goethes Amerikabild.* Zurich, 1958.
———. *Goethe in Böhmen.* 2nd ed. Zürich, 1965.
Wachsmuth, Andreas B. *Geeinte Zwienatur: Aufsätze zu Goethes wissenschaftlichem Denken.* Berlin, 1966.
———. "Goethes naturwissenschaftliche Erfahrungen und Überzeugungen in dem Roman *Wilhelm Meisters Wanderjahren.*" *Weimarer Beiträge* 6 (1960):1019–1107.
Wadepuhl, Walter. *Goethe's Interest in the New World.* 2nd ed. New York, 1973.

Waidson, Herbert Morgan. "Death by Water, or the Childhood of Wilhelm Meister." *Modern Language Review* 56 (1961):44–53.
von Wiese, Benno. "'Der Mann von funfzig Jahren.'" *Die deutsche Novelle von Goethe bis Kafka* 2:26–52.
Willoughby, L. A. "Literary Relations in the Light of Goethe's Principle of 'Wiederspiegelung.'" *Comparative Literature* 1 (1949).309–23.
———. "Namen und Namengebung bei Goethe." In *Goethe und die Tradition*. Edited by Hans Reiss. Frankfurt/M., 1972.
Wolff, Eugen. *Goethes Wilhelm Meisters Wanderjahre: Ein Novellenkranz*. Frankfurt/M., 1916.
———. "Die ursprüngliche Gestalt von *Wilhelm Meisters Wanderjahren*." *Goethejahrbuch* 34 (1913):162–92.
Wundt, Max. *Goethes Wilhelm Meister*. Berlin und Leipzig, 1913.
———. "'Aus Makariens Archiv': Zur Entstehung der Aphorismensammlung," *Germanisch-Romanische Monatsschrift* 7 (1915):177–84.
Ziolkowski, Theodore. "Die Natur als Nachahmung der Kunst bei Goethe." *Wissen aus Erfahrungen*. Festschrift für Hermann Meyer zum 65. Geburtstag. Tübingen, 1976.

INDEX

Abbé, 49, 90
actor friend. *See der theatralische Freund*
der adelige Herr, 80, 81, 91
Albertina, 48, 84, 86, 87, 88, 89, 91; *Hausfreund*, 86, 88, 91
American utopia, 10, 102, 121; emigrants to, 46, 81, 86, 102, 105, 122, 123, 142
Amtmann and labor force, 10, 82, 92, 94, 107, 121
Angela, 13, 104, 111, 112
anger and ridicule, 80, 87, 92, 87, 92; hate, 87, 92
aphorisms, 10, 20, 69, 70, 71, 80, 82, 110–18 passim; *Aus Makariens Archiv*, 20, 104, 110–18 passim, 122; *Betrachtungen im Sinne der Wanderer*, 71, 110–18 passim, 122; *das Blatt*, 122; "literary seeds," 118; maxims, 118; *Ottiliens Tagebuch*, 112; reflections, 110–18 passim
Arachne, 64, 65
archetype, 5, 16–23 passim, 32, 120, 128, 138. *See also Urform, Urbild, Urphänomen*
archive fiction, 14
art, 90, 91, 106, 107; architects, 100; artist-craftsman, 73, 90, 91; *"freie Künste,"* 90; *Kunstwerk*, 115, 118; and life, 29; as medicine, 111; music, 67, 100, 106; pedagogical value, 103; poetry, 66, 106; sketching, 67, 107; story telling, 76; *"strenge Künste,"* 90; theater, 102
astronomer, 103, 115
Aurora, 86, 88, 89. *See also* Princess Sophronie

Auswanderer, 2
autobiography, 7. *See also Dichtung und Wahrheit*

Barbier, 50, 74, 75, 76
Baroness, 62, 63, 123
basalt, 130
beautiful widow. *See schöne Witwe*
beginning, 120
Berggespräche, 82, 94–99 passim, 111, 121, 122, 123. *See also* conversations
Besteck, 70, 97, 98, 124, 127
Betrachtungen im Sinne der Wanderer. *See* aphorisms
Boisserée, Sulpiz, 15
Bourdon, Sebastien, 27
Brentano, Bettina von, 153 (n. 9)
Brieftasche, 63, 64, 65
Brion, Friederike, 74, 78

cahiers de Lecture, 34
Campagne in Frankreich, 35
Cervantes, Miguel de, 155n
Christoph, 50, 79, 80, 81, 91
contrasts, 30, 38, 48, 54, 65, 76, 78, 81, 85, 90, 91, 109, 118, 141
conversation, 69, 70, 76, 97, 98, 101, 103, 104, 108, 111, 112, 113, 114, 115, 118, 122, 142; on mathematics, 103. *See also Berggespräche*

Damenkalender. *See Taschenbuch für Damen*
Dämonen, 2; demonic, 77
Demeter, 136
denken und tun, 98
Dichtung und Wahrheit, 7, 74, 76.

INDEX

Dresden gallery, 29
Dürer, Albrecht, 27
dwarf, 75, 76, 77; parlor of, 75; princess, 75, 77, 91; race of, 75; world of, 77, 91

Eckermann, Johann Peter, 20, 25, 110
Eduard, 7
education, 56, 87, 89, 96, 97, 98, 99, 101, 105, 111, 124, 142. *See also* medical training of Wilhelm
Egmont, 20
Einwanderer, 2
Elizabeth, 24
emigrants, 81; emigration, 92; league of, 92, 105, 107, 112, 122, 123
ending, 59, 121
Entsagung, ix, 2, 12, 20, 97, 107; lack of self-control, 91; league of, 12, 107

falcon, Boccaccio's, 31, 34, 55
family, 5, 8, 29, 32, 37, 38, 45, 47, 54, 55, 57, 59, 60, 61, 66, 71, 77, 87, 88, 90, 91, 99, 101, 102, 104, 105, 120, 123, 127, 128, 131, 141, 142; family of families, 47; family tree, 61, 127; Holy Family, 32; motivation to form, 32; non-blood-related, 2282–83; property of, 67, 87, 89, 99; as *Urform* and metamorphosis, ix, 17–23 passim, 93, 99, 101, 108, 128, 138
Farbenlehre, 2, 18
fathers (and sons), 33, 34, 71, 72, 86, 88, 89, 104, 128
Faust, ix, 6, 20, 34, 128, 129, 131
Felix, 21, 31, 50, 56, 95, 96, 98, 99, 101, 114, 120, 123, 124, 128, 130, 131, 132, 139, 141

von Fellenberg, Philipp Emanuel, 101
Fischerknaben, 24, 10–16 passim, 23, 49, 50, 68–73 passim, 80, 82, 94, 109, 111, 113, 114, 121, 122
Flavio, 21, 50, 56, 58–67 passim, 78, 105, 107, 123, 139
Flight into Egypt, 24–33 passim
form, 25, 31, 55, 100, 108; cyclical, 76; loose, 31
frame, 26, 69, 70, 71, 75, 80, 84, 85, 95, 98, 99, 100, 103, 106, 108, 109, 113
Frankfurt, 71
French nobility, 37, 54
French Revolution, 2, 97
Friedrich, 13, 54, 70, 112
Fritz, 95, 128
Fromann, Johanna, 63

der Garnbote, 42
Ganymede, 127
Die gefährliche Wette, 9–16 passim, 36, 42, 49, 50, 79–83 passim, 87, 91, 114, 121, 123, 125; *Schwank*, 79; *Unregelmäßigkeit*, 79
der Gehilfe, 42, 46, 92, 108, 124
German middle class, 37, 54, 73, 81
der Geschirrfasser, 42, 92, 108
Gessner, Salomon, 46
Goethe, Johann Wolfgang von, 3, 6, 17, 24, 26, 34, 38, 39, 42, 47, 50, 58, 61, 63, 65, 68, 70, 71, 73, 74, 77, 79, 81, 82, 84, 85, 86, 87, 88, 92, 94, 95, 100, 101, 102, 104, 108, 109, 110, 113, 115, 116, 117, 118, 119, 120, 12 124, 125, 126, 127, 130, 131, 132, 133, 134, 141; agrees with Hegel, 17, 19; art collection of, 27, 29; as *Augen-*

mensch, 27; defines novelle, 11; interest in families of, 17; as monotheist, polytheist, pantheist, 4; powers of in old age, ix
gold, 131
goldsmith and jeweler, 130
granite, 95, 130
Gulliver's Travels, 127
die Gute-Schöne, 45–51 passim. See also Nachodine, Susanne, *Die Schöne-Gute*

Haller, Albrecht von, 46
hate. See anger
Hegel, G. W. F.: Goethe agrees with, 19; *Philosophie des Geistes und Rechtsphilosophie*, 17, 18, 19, 20; philosophy of law, 99, 101; *Phänomenologie des Geistes*, 17, 18, 19, 99, 142; reacts to Goethe's *Farbentheorie*, 18; visits Goethe, 19
Die Heimsuchung, 25–33 passim. See also St. Joseph II
Herder, Johann Gottfried von, 139
Hersilie, 13, 34, 36, 42, 50, 53, 58, 65, 102, 114, 123, 128, 130, 131, 132, 133, 139
Herzlieb, Minna, 153
Hilarie, 50, 58, 59, 60, 61, 62, 65, 66, 67, 105, 106, 107, 123, 124, 139
Hofmarschall, 65

Icherzählung, 25, 70, 81, 84, 87
Iken, Karl J. L., 14
inferiors, 30, 33, 48, 56, 65, 77, 81, 88. See also superiors
Iphigenia, 127
irony, 30, 60, 62, 87

Jagdgedicht, 64
Jarno, 21, 22, 94, 97. See also Montan

Joseph II. See St. Joseph II
Joseph II, Emperor of Austria, 27
Julie, 52, 57
Juliette, 37, 42, 53, 54, 123
Junker, 52, 53
Jupiter, 104

Kanzler Müller, 59, 147
Karl August, 134
Kästchen, 12, 113, 114, 126, 129, 130, 131, 132, 133, 134, 135, 136; *cista mystica*, 134, 135, 136; κιστή, 135, 136, 138; rings, 136
Katzengold, 96
key, 126–35 passim, 141; exotic elements, 129, 133; handle, 133, 138; magnetic joint, 129, 130; phallic symbol, 129, 133; Seventh Commandment, 129; shaft, 133; two circles, 134. See also Schlüsselroman
Kleist, Ewald von, 46
Kohlenmeiler, 69, 97, 99
Kotzebue, August Friedrich Ferdinand von, 153 (n. 1)
Aus Kunst und Altertum, 27; *Kunst und Altertum am Rhein und Main*, 154n

Lago Maggiore, 10, 58, 67, 82, 94, 103, 106–7, 121, 123; Isola Bella, 106
left-handed heroes, 80, 125
Lehrjahre: Bekenntnisse einer schönen Seele, 35, 56, 68, 70, 94, 97, 106, 139; innovative, viii, 21, 22, 24, 34, 46
Lenardo, 2, 21, 39–51 passim, 68, 70, 75, 78, 86, 88, 90, 92, 94, 102, 107, 112, 120, 123, 124, 139, 142; *als Band*, 49; *Fortsetzung*, 45–48, 59, 67, 82, 91, 95; *Leidenschaft aus Gewissen*, 43,

INDEX

47, 142; *Lenardos Archiv*, 54, 80; St. Leonard, 40; second hero of *Wanderjahre*, 51; *Tagebuch*, 44, 45, 59, 70, 82, 95; *Wanderrede*, 121, 123
Levetzow, Ulrike von, 153
lightness-darkness, 63, 98, 99, 101
Der Lilienstengel, 24–33 passim. *See also* St. Joseph II
Linkage: between parts, 41, 86, 87; external, 29, 41, 58, 69, 75, 80, 86; internal, 29, 31, 37, 41, 58, 59, 68, 69, 77, 81, 87; of *Novellen* to main plot, 12, 29, 120
Lothario, 22
loyalty, 35; constancy, 107; disloyalty, 35, 91, 121
Lucidor, 37, 38, 52–57 passim, 78, 87, 123, 124, 128, 139
Lucinde, 39, 53, 124, 128, 139
Lusignan, 74
Lydie, 106

main plot, 25, 29, 30, 36, 41, 70, 77, 85, 86, 93, 94, 101, 102, 108, 109, 120, 125
Major, 50, 56, 58–67 passim, 78, 105, 107, 123, 139
Makarie, 10, 13, 22, 43, 44, 63, 68, 73, 82, 94, 102–6 passim, 111, 112, 114, 115, 121, 122, 123, 124; archive, 103, 114; *Aus Makariens Archiv*, 20; causes *Steigerung*, 103, 104, 105; girls' school, 104, 124; Makarie II, 103; secular saint, 105; sees core of a person, 103; and solar system, 103. *See also* aphorisms
Mann, Thomas, 20
Der Mann von funfzig Jahren, 2, 9, 10, 36, 37, 49, 50, 55, 56, 58–67 passim, 78, 80, 82, 87, 102, 103, 105, 109, 120, 121, 123, 124, 127, 142
Maria, 32
Mariane, 22
marriage, 29, 76, 77, 78, 87, 88, 107; broken, 85; ideal, 85, 87; for power and prestige, 85, 87; negative model, 85; of a ruler, 77, 78, 88
medical training of Wilhelm, 10, 50, 56, 68, 69, 72, 82, 87, 94, 98, 113, 121, 122, 124
Melina, 22
metamorphosis, 5, 8, 17–23 passim, 32, 43, 45, 59, 66, 68, 72, 93, 99, 120, 124, 141, 142; accidental, 123, 141; normal, 123, 141; regressive, 123, 141, 142
Metternich, 92
Meyer, Heinrich, 32, 35, 48
Mignon, 106, 107
Minerva, 64
monologue, 53, 55
Montan, 2, 10, 69, 82, 94–99 passim, 111, 121, 122, 124. *See also* Jarno
mountaintop, 94–99 passim
Der Müllerin Verrat, 35
Musenalmanach, 35
music, 76, 77

Nachodine, 39, 40, 41, 68, 142. *See also* Susanne, *die Gute-Schöne, die Schöne-Gute*
narrative insertions, 34, 42, 50, 55, 65, 68, 76, 78, 79, 84, 86, 92, 94–109 passim, 110, 113, 114, 115, 118, 120, 121, 122, 142; continuum of, 109; narrative strands, 85; series of, ix; titled, 108, 109, 122; untitled, 99, 108, 109, 122. *See also* novella

narrator, 74, 75, 76, 84, 91
Natalie, 21, 31, 48, 69, 70, 107, 128, 139
negative example, 38, 75, 78, 80, 82, 83, 84, 88, 91, 108, 121, 123, 124, 142. *See also* metamorphosis
negative stimulus, 40, 50
Die neue Melusine, 36, 46, 48, 49, 55, 74–78 passim, 80, 81, 88, 91, 114, 121, 123, 125, 141, 142; *die schöne Melusine*, 74
Nicht zu weit, 36, 46, 48, 49, 50, 55, 66, 78, 82, 84–93 passim, 108, 121, 123, 124, 141, 142
nobility, 80. *See also* French nobility
novel, 31, 33, 38, 79, 81, 82, 85, 91, 92, 94, 96, 99, 102, 105, 106, 108, 111, 113, 118, 125, 126, 127, 141, 143; *Bildungsroman*, 12
novella, 6, 9–16 passim, 29, 36, 38, 52, 56, 57, 58, 59, 79, 81, 84, 85, 89, 94, 99, 108, 120, 140; definition of, 11; groups of three, 121; Italian or French model, 34; legend, 76; *Märchen*, 74; titled, 81, 82, 93, 94; two groups, 36; untitled, 81, 82, 99–109 passim; various names for, 3, 11; with love story, 81, 82, 121; without love story, 81, 82, 121
Das nußbraune Mädchen, 10, 39–51 passim, 55, 58, 65, 68, 78, 80, 91, 94, 121, 141, 142

Odoardo, 13, 48, 50, 84–93 passim, 107, 108, 120, 124, 139; despotism of, 90, 93; marriage of, 87; philistinism of, 91; recruiting speech of, 86, 122; as reform-minded conservative, 84; and respect for authority, 84, 85

Oedipus, 98
offenbares Geheimnis, 127, 128, 131
Ottilie's journal. *See* aphorisms
Ovid, 64

Die pädogogische Provinz, 12, 50, 56, 79, 82, 87, 94, 96, 98, 99–102 passim, 111, 112, 121, 122, 123, 124, 133, 142; three reverences, 79
painter from Lago Maggiore, 13, 106, 107
painting collections, 24, 26, 27, 29, 57, 100, 103, 106, 124, 127
pantheism, 4, 72, 95, 143. *See also* Spinoza
parallel, 30, 54, 65, 80, 98, 109; *Parallelgeschichten*, 14, 122; parallel tradition, 30
Paulinzella, 26
Penelope, 64
perspective, 1, 31, 82, 85
Pfeile, 131, 138
Philine, 106
physician, 68, 69; *Arzt*, 72, 73; *Chirung*, 73; *Leibarzt*, 73; *Seelenarzt*, 73; *Wundarzt*, 70, 73, 75
Die pilgernde Törin, 10, 12, 31, 34, 38, 42, 49, 50, 53, 54, 65, 82, 121, 123, 139, 141
Plato, 29
polarity, 6, 38, 78, 140, 141
positive model, 93. *See also* St. Joseph II
Princess Sophronie, 88. *See also* Aurora
profession, 29, 70, 72, 97, 98; anatomical models, 73; craft, 30, 96, 97; dissection, 73

Raufbold, 81, 92
renunciation. *See Entsagung*
Revannes, father and son, 34, 35, 123

INDEX   169

ridicule. *See* anger
Rochus-Festival at Bingen, 20
Romanze, 35
Ruderpflock, 69, 70, 113, 127
Ruysdael, Jakob, 27, 28

St. Joseph II, 10, 12, 19, 24–33 passim, 36, 39, 41, 42, 48, 55, 69, 70, 78, 82, 85, 86, 87, 93, 94, 120, 121, 127, 128, 139, 141; as representative of Middle Ages, 1
St. Luke, 24
Der Sammler, 2, 42, 108, 109, 123, 129
Sankt Joseph der Zweite, 24–33 passim. *See also* St. Joseph II
Saxe-Weimar, 85, 86; Eisenach, 85; enclaves in, 86
Schiller, Friedrich von, 12, 35, 74
Schlosser, 85
Schlüsselroman, 126. *See also* key
die *Schöne-Gute*, 39–51 passim; *kalokagathia*, 41. *See also* Nachodine, Susanne, die *Gute-Schöne*
die schöne *Witwe*, 58, 59, 62, 63, 64, 65, 67, 105, 106, 107, 124, 139
Schuchardt, Christian, 27
science, 4, 72, 81, 116, 118, 119, 120, 125; anatomy, 128; botany, 72, 119; botany and the family, 17; compatible with poetry, 5; geology, 72, 98; origin of earth, 98, 101; mineralogy, 119; morphology, 119; natural science, 4; optics, 119; osteology, 128; science patterns in poetry, 6; scientific notebook, 48; zoology, 119
Sein und Schein, 62, 111
self-control, 76, 78
series, 2, 8, 17, 81, 93, 115, 119–25 passim, 142; accidental metamorphosis, 5; developmental series, 119; intermaxillary bone, 119; normal-abnormal series, 119; regressive metamorphosis, 5; regular metamorphosis, 5; series of series, 125
Sesenheim, 74, 78
sexual symbol, 131, 133, 134, 138, 139; basket, 134; birth, 132; Demeter, 133; phallus, 131, 133, 134; womb, 132
sexuality, 139
Sinn auf!, 98
socialists, 17
spinners, 45, 50, 82
Spinoza, Baruch, 4. *See also* pantheism
Steigerung, 6, 47, 104, 105, 106, 142; *steigern*, 90
superiors, 30, 33, 48, 56, 57, 65, 77, 81, 88. *See also* inferiors
Susanne, 38–51 passim; her father, 46, 49; feeling for *das Volk*, 48–49, 66, 88, 92, 108, 124. *See also* Nachodine, die *Gute-Schöne*, die *Schöne-Gute*

Taschenbuch für Damen, 25
der theatralische Freund, 61, 62
Therese, 22
third-person narrative, 87
tree of knowledge, 131
Treue, 35
triangle pictures: Lenardo, Susanne, Gehilfe, 46, 66, 120; *Mann von 50 Jahre*, 61, 66, 120; *Nicht zu weit*, 46, 66, 84, 120; *Wer ist der Verräter?*, 56, 120; Wilhelm, Felix, Hersilie, 139
Tristram Shandy, 127
Tun und Denken, 98, 101, 111

Übermut, 79

uncle, 39, 102, 109, 111, 122, 123, 124
Die Unterhaltungen deutscher Ausgewanderten, 14
Urbild, 5, 16–23 passim, 30, 32. See also archetype, *Urform*, *Urphänomen*
Urform, 5, 16–23 passim, 30, 59, 72, 93, 120, 125; painting becomes, 29, 32. See also archetype, *Urbild*, *Urphänomen*
Urphänomen, 5, 16–23 passim, 142. See also archetype, *Urform*, *Urbild*

Valerine, 42, 43
Virgin Mary, 29
Volk, 20, 54, 56, 57, 65, 66, 67, 68, 82, 88, 101, 102, 141; family of families, 17, 45, 47; *Volkheit*, 20; *Völkerschaft*, 45
Vulpius, Christiane, 139

Wahlverwandtschaften, 7, 66, 112, 125, 139; more traditional novel, 1
Wanderjahre, viii, 2, 14, 21, 56, 68, 84, 91, 97, 99, 127, 132, 133, 139, 143; departure from tradition, viii; 1821 version, viii, 11, 25, 49, 54, 58, 59, 65, 79, 98, 127; *Entsagung*, ix; *Entwicklungsroman*, 12; errors in, viii; experimental novel, 12; Faust and *Wanderjahre*, viii, ix; found no audience, viii; as novel, ix; novel of perspectives, ix, 82; scientific structure of, ix
weavers, 44, 45, 46, 47, 50, 84, 101, 123, 124, 140; mechanical looms, 46, 48, 50; stocking weavers of Apolda, 47; *Die Weber*, 47
Weimar, 86
Wer ist der Verräter?, 10, 36, 37, 46, 48, 49, 52–57 passim, 76, 78, 82, 87, 99, 103, 108, 109, 121, 123, 124, 140
Werther, 126
West-Östlicher Divan, 35
widowed princess, 65
Wiederholte Spiegelungen, 2, 14, 30, 55, 120, 130, 141; Iken letter to, 14
Wilhelm, 10, 21, 22, 24, 25, 26, 29, 30, 31, 41, 42, 43, 44, 48, 50, 53, 54, 56, 58, 65, 68–73 passim, 87, 94, 95, 96, 99, 100, 101, 103, 104, 105, 107, 112, 113, 114, 122, 123, 124, 127, 128, 129, 130, 139, 141; aunt, 71; *das Blatt*, 122; father, 22; vision, 104
von Willemer, Marianne, 35
wounds, 37, 43, 56, 68
Württemberg, 86

Ziegesaar, Sylvie von, 153
Zelter, Karl Friedrich, 16, 19
Zwischenrede, 11, 15, 100

www.ingramcontent.com/pod-product-compliance
Lightning Source LLC
Chambersburg PA
CBHW020802160426
43192CB00006B/411